Everyday Life:
MIDDLE AGES

WITH CROSS-CURRICULAR ACTIVITIES IN EACH CHAPTER

WALTER A. HAZEN

A GOOD YEAR BOOK™

GOOD YEAR BOOKS

Tucson, Arizona

Photo Credits

Front & back cover: All images owned by Good Year Books. 2: Roman aqueduct, Bridgeman Art Library. 4: Lithograph of Viking warrior, Bridgeman Art Library. 5: King Charles V, Bridgeman Art Library. 10: Vellum artwork, Bridgeman Art Library. 12: Illuminated manuscript, Bridgeman Art Library. 13: Early football, Bridgeman Art Library. 18: Bodiam castle, Good Year Books. 20: Bayeux Tapestry, Bridgeman Art Library. 21: Chess game, Bridgeman Art Library. 27: Knighting, Bridgeman Art Library. 28: Three knights, Bridgeman Art Library. 34: King Arthur, Bridgeman Art Library. 36: St. George and the Dragon, Bridgeman Art Library. 37: Unicorn, Bridgeman Art Library. 42: Ruins of Irish church, Bridgeman Art Library. 44: Holy Roman Emperor Henry IV and Pope Gregory, Bridgeman Art Library. 45: Illuminated manuscript, Bridgeman Art Library. 50: Jousting at a tournament, Bridgeman Art Library. 52: Falconer, Bridgeman Art Library. 53: Medieval fair, Bridgeman Art Library. 58: Peter the Hermit, Bridgeman Art Library. 60: Children's Crusade, Bridgeman Art Library. 61: Crusader, Bridgeman Art Library. 66: Plague victims, Bridgeman Art Library. 68: Monteriggioni, Bridgeman Art Library. 69: Guild master and journeyman, Bridgeman Art Library. 75: University of Bologna, Bridgeman Art Library. 76: Medieval students, Bridgeman Art Library. 77: Students at University of Bologna, Bridgeman Art Library. 82: Fresco of alchemist, Bridgeman Art Library. 83: Dante Alighieri, Bridgeman Art Library. 85: Cathedral at Chartres, Bridgeman Art Library.

Dedication

To Martha, Jordan, and Allison.

Acknowledgments

Grateful acknowledgment is extended to Roberta Dempsey, Editorial Director at Good Year Books, who patiently guided me through this addition to the "Everyday Life" series. Without her advice and support, this book would not have been possible.

I would also like to thank Helen Fisher, Publisher at Good Year Books, for giving me the opportunity to continue the "Everyday Life" series. Her support and confidence in me is likewise appreciated.

Good Year Books

are available for most basic curriculum subjects plus many enrichment areas. For more Good Year Books, contact your local bookseller or educational dealer. For a complete catalog with information about other Good Year Books, please contact:

Good Year Books
P. O. Box 91858
Tucson, Arizona 85752-1858
1-800-511-1530
www.goodyearbooks.com

Editor: Roberta Dempsey
Cover Design: Ronan Design
Interior Design: Dan Miedaner

ISBN-10: 1-59647-059-3
ISBN-13: 978-1-59647-059-0

1 2 3 4 5 6 7 8 9 - BN - 07 06 05

Table of Contents

Table of Contents *continued*

Introduction

In AD 476, the western half of the once-great Roman Empire came to an
end. This came after years of attacks and invasions by "barbarian" tribes,
as the Romans called the Germanic, Celtic, and Slavic peoples to their
north and west. The Eastern Roman Empire survived in Constantinople (now
called Istanbul) until 1453, becoming known as the Byzantine Empire. After
the fall of Rome, European towns were destroyed, roads fell into disrepair, and
trade and travel came to a halt. What followed was some three hundred to five
hundred years of disorder and confusion, often referred to as the *Dark Ages.*
This period made up the early part of the *Middle Ages,* beginning with the fall
of Rome and reaching its peak in the 1200s. Most scholars put the end of the
Middle Ages around 1500, a time when great changes took place around the
world.

Everyday Life: The Middle Ages deals with all the familiar things that come
to mind when one thinks of the period: knights, castles, manors, tournaments,
the Crusades, and the like. It is filled with interesting stories and anecdotes that
help to make the people of the age real and personable. As with earlier books in
the series, each chapter ends with activities that span the school curriculum. In
addition to those that focus on social studies, there are other activities that deal
with math, drama, critical thinking, grammar, and cooking, to name a few.

Because of space limitations, *Everyday Life: The Middle Ages* focuses almost
entirely on Europe. This is not to say that important events were not happening
in other parts of the world. On the contrary, while Europe was engulfed in
warfare in the Dark Ages, great civilizations were flourishing elsewhere. Mighty
African kingdoms such as Ghana, Mali, and Songhai made notable achievements
in the years covered by the European Middle Ages. So too did civilizations in
China, India, and what later came to be called Latin America. In the latter, the
great Mayan civilization, for example, had existed long before the birth of
Christ, to be followed by those of the Aztecs and Incas. And, from reading the
text of this book, the student will learn how the Arab civilizations of the
Middle East had such a great impact on ushering in modern times in Europe.

Everyday Life: The Middle Ages is a book that students should find
informative, interesting, and entertaining.

Walter A. Hazen

CHAPTER I

The Feudal System

The year is 1015. You live with your family on a manor, or large estate, in rural France. Because it is a warm spring evening, you decide to hitch up a cart and visit a friend who lives on another manor a short distance to the south. You whistle happily as you wave good-bye to your parents and proceed down the cobblestone road.

What is wrong with the above scenario? Several things. If you guessed that no one—child or adult—would venture out alone in the year 1015, you are correct. If you further guessed that most people who lived on manors were serfs with neither access to a cart nor permission to leave of their own free will, you are right again. And if you pointed out that there may or may not have been a decent road, you are extremely clever!

One of many aqueducts constructed by the Romans. Some Roman aqueducts are still in use today.

There is nothing particularly significant about the year 1015. It was just one year in a period of the Middle Ages known as *feudal times.* The word *feudal* refers to "feudalism," the economic, political, and social system that characterized medieval Europe from about 1000 to 1300. Here is how it all came about.

For more than a thousand years, a people known as the Romans controlled most of Europe and all the lands bordering on the Mediterranean Sea. They built magnificent buildings and constructed fine roads. Some of their roads are still in use today, as are some of the aqueducts they used to transport water. Aqueducts were bridge-like structures that carried water to cities throughout the far-flung world of the Romans.

The Romans were as skilled at government administration as they were at building things. From the city of Rome to the outlying provinces, efficient government and just laws made for an orderly society. This was particularly true during the first two hundred years of Rome's empire period, extending from about 27 BC to AD 180. Taxes were collected and manufacturing and trade flourished. People in general were happy and traveled about the empire without fear for their safety.

From *Everyday Life: The Middle Ages* © 2006 Good Year Books.

But then, as the old saying goes, "the bottom fell out." Within the Roman Empire, economic conditions deteriorated and citizens lost interest in civic affairs. Civil wars became the order of the day, and the army installed one emperor after another on the throne. Twenty-five emperors were murdered within one fifty-year period.

Outside the empire, the sinking of land in northern Europe and pressure from Asian peoples to the east set off mass migrations across the borders of the Roman Empire. It took more than two hundred years, but in AD 476, one tribe, the Visigoths, conquered the city of Rome. Although the eastern part of the Roman Empire continued for another thousand years, in the west the Roman Empire came to an end.

The fall of Rome led to the development of feudalism. Many Germans had lived under Roman rule or had been allies of the Romans against other invaders. In fact, the leader of the Visigoths who conquered Rome was Odoacer, a German who was serving as a general in the Roman army. But Europe was living in a state of almost continual warfare, and few people wrote accounts of the time. Because we know so little about this period of history, people call the period the *Dark Ages*.

For the most part, the Germans and Celts lived in tribes under local rulers. But in the eighth century, one Germanic king managed to bring much of Europe under his control. That king was Charlemagne, or "Charles the Great," the first Holy Roman Emperor. Charlemagne was king of a German tribe known as the *Franks*. Does that name ring a bell? It should. It is from *Franks* that the name *France* is derived.

Charlemagne ruled from 768 to 814. During his long reign, there was stability in western Europe. But when Charlemagne died, his grandsons were unable to keep his empire together. The result was a breakdown in central government again, although Charlemagne's laws survived as the basis for the medieval kingdoms of France and Germany.

Matters were made even worse by the regular invasions of the Vikings. Also known as the Northmen or Norsemen, Viking pirates swept out of Scandinavia (Norway, Sweden, and Denmark) in the ninth century, raiding and plundering. The accounts of the Vikings that survive come from the monasteries that were the targets of their raids. A common prayer of the time was, "From the fury of the Northmen, O Lord, deliver us!"

Although remarkably democratic and civil among themselves, the Vikings were very warlike, showing no sympathy for the people they attacked. They

killed women and children with their long-handled axes just as easily as they killed men. After looting and then burning everything in sight, they sailed home in their long, sleek boats.

The lack of a central government led to the development of the feudal system mentioned earlier. This feudal system grew out of people's need for protection. With no strong kings to maintain law and order, people turned to local lords for help. At the heart of the system were personal arrangements between two parties.

Lithograph of a Viking warrior. The Vikings terrorized Europe in the early Middle Ages.

Feudal arrangements involved kings, powerful lords, and lesser nobles. Even though kings had little power, they were still kings, and on occasion they needed to raise an army, as did dukes and nobles. To do so, they granted tracts of land to the lords beneath them. A king or lord who gave land to a lesser lord became the latter's overlord. The one receiving the land became the vassal of the one who granted it. The land itself was called a *fief*.

A vassal who received land from a king or higher lord was obligated to fight for him for a certain number of days a year. If the vassal himself had vassals, they were obligated to fight also. Specially trained warriors called *knights*, lived in the castles or manor houses of great lords, or received a knight's fee, usually enough land to yield 20 pounds income a year. They paid for their keep by serving in the lord's army. In a later chapter, you will read about training to become a knight. For now, it is enough to say that only after successfully passing through the ranks of page and squire did a young man attain knighthood.

Sometimes feudal arrangements and agreements were quite complicated. It was not unusual for a person to be a vassal to two or more lords at the same time. Having received a fief from each, he was therefore obligated to serve both. This posed no problem unless his two overlords went to war against each other! Sometimes the vassal's contract would say what he was to do. For example, he might have to fight for one lord but send a number of his knights to fight on the other side!

A vassal had responsibilities other than to serve his lord in battle. He also had to sit on the lord's court, where he might judge the guilt or innocence of

From *Everyday Life: The Middle Ages* © 2006 Good Year Books.

another vassal. If his lord stopped by for a visit, the vassal had to provide food and shelter for his superior and all of his party. Not the least of the vassal's promises was to help pay the ransom demanded when his lord was unfortunate enough to get himself captured by an enemy.

The lord/vassal relationship was a serious arrangement not to be taken lightly. It was initiated with great ceremony at the castle or manor house of the lord. The vassal knelt before his lord and placed his hands between the hands of the lord. He then solemnly swore that he would honor all the commitments expected of a vassal. This formal acknowledgment on the part of the vassal was called "doing homage." At the lord's demand, this ceremony, with its accompanying promise of allegiance, was repeated.

Technically, the peasantry were not part of the feudal system, because they were not warriors. They lived a hard life under the manorial system, which existed even before feudalism. Some were serfs, who were actually bound to the land. If the land was sold, the serfs went along with it as part of the deal. Others were freedmen, tenant farmers who paid the lord in money and a portion of their crops for the right to work the land. The lord gave his serfs and tenants protection and they turned to him for justice. In exchange, the lord charged taxes, required labor, took some of the crops, and generally made sure that the peasants were too poor to leave the land.

In this painting, King Charles V presents his sword to one of his vassals. A king's vassal was obligated to fight for his lord for a certain number of days a year.

Last, not every knight was a vassal to a lord. This was especially true toward the end of the feudal period. Some knights hired themselves out to the highest bidder for their services. They were known as mercenary knights. Mercenary knights were more professional soldiers than true knights. They became important toward the end of the feudal period when kings and lords started having difficulty rounding up enough knights to fight for them.

As you have seen, feudalism was a complicated system of agreements made between lords and vassals. But it served its purpose in an age characterized by a lack of government.

Name _____ Date _____

Create a Dialogue

Our brave French knight, Sir Gallant, is faced with a dilemma. He has the misfortune of being a vassal to both the Count of Rouen and the Count of Amiens, who, as luck would have it, are about to settle an argument over a piece of land on the field of battle. Both counts send out a call for their vassals and their vassals' knights to assemble immediately for the purpose of forming an army.

What is Sir Gallant to do? Can he choose to support one count at the expense of the other? Can he somehow serve both? How is he to make use of the four knights in his service? He is, in modern slang terminology, "caught between a rock and a hard place."

On the lines opposite, create a dialogue between Sir Gallant and his wife, Jeanne, as they discuss what he should best do. Write any solution you may have to the problem into the course of their conversation.

From *Everyday Life: The Middle Ages* © 2006 Good Year Books.

Name _____   Date _____

Recall Information You Have Read

How well do you remember what you read? The ability to recall information is a learning skill that grows in importance as you advance from one grade to the next in school.

Without looking back over the chapter, define or identify as best you can the names and terms listed below.

1. feudalism
_____
_____

2. vassal
_____
_____

3. overlord
_____
_____

4. fief
_____
_____

5. homage
_____
_____

6. Vikings
_____
_____

7. serf
_____
_____

8. aqueduct
_____
_____

9. Visigoths
_____
_____

10. Charlemagne
_____
_____

Name _____ Date _____

Solve a Feudalism Puzzle

Fill in the sentences for clues to complete the puzzle about feudalism.

```
F _ _ _
_ E _ _ _
_ _ U _ _ _ _ _
_ _ _ _ _ _ _ D _ _
_ A _ _ _ _
_ _ _ _ L _ _ _ _
_ _ I _ _ _
_ _ S _ _ _
_ _ M _ _ _
```

1. A piece of land granted by one lord to another was called a _____.

2. A _____ was a peasant bound to the soil.

3. An _____ was a structure that carried water to a Roman city.

4. A lord who granted land to another lord was called an _____.

5. A _____ received land from another lord.

6. _____ was a famous king of the Franks.

7. The _____ who raided Europe came from Scandinavia.

8. Rome fell in the year 476 to a German tribe called the _____.

9. A vassal paid _____, or promised allegiance, to an overlord.

From Everyday Life: The Middle Ages © 2006 Good Year Books.

Name _____   Date _____

Do a Scan of Scandinavia

You read in chapter I that the Vikings came from the Scandinavian countries of Norway, Sweden, and Denmark. But the term *Scandinavia* is often used to refer to all countries where Scandinavian people live. This would include Finland and Iceland as well as Norway, Sweden, and Denmark.

With this information in mind, consult an encyclopedia or some other source and answer these questions.

1. What is the origin of the word *Scandinavia*?

   _____

   _____

   _____

2. What are the capitals of the five countries considered to be part of Scandinavia?

   Norway _____   Sweden _____

   Denmark _____   Finland _____

   Iceland _____

3. Between which two Scandinavian countries does the Gulf of Bothnia lie?

   _____ and _____.

4. Southern Sweden and eastern Denmark are bordered by the _____ Sea.

5. The North Sea borders the western part of the Scandinavian country of _____.

6. Finland is bordered on the east by the nation of _____.

7. The country bordering Denmark to the south is _____.

8. Iceland lies in the middle of the North _____ Ocean.

9. Citizens of the United States are called Americans. What are the people who live in Finland called? _____

   In Norway? _____

   In Denmark? _____

   In Iceland? _____

   In Sweden? _____

CHAPTER 2

Life on a Manor

Life in the Middle Ages centered around the manor, or large estate, of a feudal lord. The wealthier lords lived in large castles. But most lived in manor houses. The size of a lord's manor house depended on his wealth.

Clustered around or near the castle or manor house were the huts and shops of the serfs and freemen who worked for the lord. Together with a chapel and a mill, these structures made up a small village. Beyond the village were the lord's fields, pasture land, and woods for hunting. Most manors in the Middle Ages were laid out in this fashion.

This vellum artwork shows serfs at work on a medieval manor.

Because some sources estimate that 90 percent of Europe's population during feudal times was made up of peasants, they are the focal point of this chapter. While the lord and his family in their castle or manor house enjoyed all the comforts associated with their position, the peasant and his family struggled just to survive. (The daily life of the noble class is covered in detail in chapter 3, "Castle Life.")

As mentioned in chapter 1, there were two types of peasants: freedmen and serfs. Freedmen had higher status because they were not bound to anyone, but their lives were nearly as hard as serfs' lives. With bandits and invaders roaming the countryside, looting and killing at will, peasants had no way of defending themselves. Thus, many entered into contracts with powerful lords. In return for the right to seek safety inside the walls of the lord's castle or manor house in times of trouble, many peasants agreed that they (and their descendants) would become serfs and work the fields of their protectors. They also agreed to give their lords a certain percentage of the crops they grew on the land they rented as tenant farmers, as well as some of the livestock they raised.

But serfs were not slaves. They had certain rights that slaves never enjoyed. One was the right to strips of land on which they met their needs for food, clothing, and shelter. After meeting their own needs and the amount due the lord, they could sell the rest. Another was a guarantee that they could not be sold separately from the land they were bound to. Serfs were as much a part of a lord's land as were all the buildings and fields. If a lord sold his estate to another lord, the serfs quite naturally went along as part of the deal.

From *Everyday Life: The Middle Ages* © 2006 Good Year Books.

Throughout the feudal period, farmers used the three-field method of farming. One field was planted in autumn, usually in wheat or rye. A second field was planted in spring, this time either in barley for making beer (water was often unfit to drink in those days) or in beans, peas, and oats. A third field was left fallow, or unplanted. The purpose of the latter was to preserve the fertility of the soil. Each year a different field was left fallow. It was plowed but not planted.

The serfs' strips of land were spread throughout these three fields. Some serfs owned only a small amount of land, but others possessed as much as 30 acres. Serfs were usually free to work their own fields three days a week. The rest of the week, except for Sunday, was given over to the lord's land. On his own strips, the serf could grow fresh vegetables or whatever he wished. But he was required to give a certain portion of his harvest to his lord. The lord also received a portion of the serf's chickens, pigs, and livestock.

The serf's duties extended beyond the lord's fields. He might have to run errands for his lord's lady, and he certainly had to have his grain ground in the lord's mill—for a fee. The same held true for the lord's oven for baking and his winepress for turning grapes into wine. The serf had to cut his firewood and hay on the lord's land and give a portion to his lord. In times of extra work, such as building, planting, or harvesting, the serf could be called on to haul stone, plow, sow, and harvest.

There is more. The serf's agreement with his lord required him to give extra on feast days. For example, at Christmas, he might have to give one of his best fowl, on Palm Sunday to come forward with a sheep, and on Easter with five eggs. Serfs hardly ever had a minute to rest. Even so, Sundays, feast days, and perhaps a week at Easter and Christmas were holidays. On these days, he gathered with fellow serfs and their families for sports and other activities. (These and other amusements are covered later in the chapter.)

Serfs' wives and daughters also worked hard. When not laboring in the fields alongside the menfolk, they helped out in the manor house. They spun cloth and made clothing. They baked bread and brewed beer. These tasks were in addition to those they were expected to perform in their own huts.

At the end of the serf's long workday, he retired to his humble hut. The typical hut was built of wood and had one or two rooms, with rushes covering the dirt floor, and a thatched roof. If it had windows at all, they were only slits covered with oiled cloths. In the center was a hearth for cooking and heat. With no chimney, smoke went out a hole in the roof. More than one hut went

up in flames because of this not-too-satisfactory arrangement. Because the thatched roofs of the huts were easily set on fire, cooking was often done outside when the weather was good.

Serfs produced their own food, which was just as plain as the quarters in which they lived. They ate a diet of black bread and vegetables such as cabbage, carrots, and onions. They also had dairy products and some pork. Water was usually unsafe to drink, so they drank mostly ale. They had no sugar, no potatoes, no tea, and no coffee. They did have salt, but only in limited amounts. They seldom ate meat.

This detail from a twelfth-century illuminated manuscript shows peasants using scythes to cut hay.

Contrary to what some people might believe, the short life expectancy of the average serf (some thirty years) probably had little to do with diet. Black bread is chock-full of vitamins and nutrients, and no one ever died early from eating cabbage and garden vegetables. And, from what we now know about nutrition and health, serfs were better off not eating a lot of meat. Their short lives were probably due to hard work and the total absence of hygiene and sanitation. The latter gave rise to diseases that took the lives of many on the manor— serf and lord alike.

Men of all ranks wore tunics, with the length of the tunic and the brightness of its colors signifying rank. Serfs wore a short woolen or sheepskin tunic and trousers that were held secure by either knee-high stockings or leggings of thin leather. The tunic had sleeves and slipped over the head like a sweatshirt. The serf also wore either a belt or a piece of rope that kept the tunic in place around the waist. He completed his attire with leather boots. In winter he added an animal skin cloak and woolen gloves and hat. The serf's wife dressed similarly but for a skirt in place of trousers.

Daughters dressed like their mothers, and sons dressed like their fathers. Many years would pass before the clothing of children ceased to be smaller versions of those of their parents.

After a week of hard work, the serf and his family looked forward to Sunday. Sundays and feast days were days of rest and amusement. Serfs got

From *Everyday Life: The Middle Ages* © 2006 Good Year Books.

together and sang, danced, and played games. One game that was popular among boisterous young men was an early kind of soccer between two towns, called mob football. It was played in the streets, and, considering the amount of ale the players had drunk beforehand, tended to get a little rough. Broken bones and gouged eyes were commonplace, and sometimes players were killed. The game became so rough that church officials outlawed it in some places.

But it mattered little if football was banned. There were other sporting activities to keep roughnecks occupied. They wrestled, had weight-lifting contests, and engaged in anything that afforded them competition. To the hard-working serf, Sundays and feast days were a time to "let off steam."

Occasionally a serf who could no longer endure conditions on the manor would run away. To do so was chancy at best. In the early part of the feudal era when few towns existed, there was really no place to run. In addition, life outside the manor was dangerous, and a runaway serf ran the risk of being killed. There was also the certainty that if he was captured and returned to his lord, he would be subjected to the cruelest of punishments.

An early form of football, which was played in the streets. Players were often seriously injured and sometimes killed.

When more towns began to appear in the thirteenth century, rulers declared that any serf who ran away and hid for a year and a day was said to be a free person. Many serfs gained their independence in this manner. Others became free when their lords were killed on crusades to the Holy Land (you will learn about these expeditions in a later chapter). And even more were able to buy their freedom when the Black Death, a terrible disease that raged through Europe, killed one-third of the continent's population. With the labor force so reduced, serfs were able to bargain for their freedom or at least for more rights in return for working the land.

Name _____ Date _____

Make Inferences from Facts

Do you know what it means to "read between the lines"? Everything we learn is not spelled out in the paragraphs of a text. Certain information is hinted at or inferred. When we learn through inferring, we use our process of reasoning to study the facts and draw conclusions about what the author is trying to say.

Read each of these statements or paragraphs. Then, on the lines provided, write what inferences you arrived at.

1. Most serfs labored six days a week on the manor. Jacques and his brother Guillaume were no exception. But their cousin, Georges, was a blacksmith on the manor, and one of their uncles, Auguste, was a miller. A close friend, Henri, was a tanner.

   _____

   _____

2. Even had serfs been able to read, there were no newspapers available during medieval times. In addition, serfs seldom traveled more than 5 miles from their respective manors, living their entire lives there.

   _____

   _____

3. In contrast to his serfs, the lord of the manor, when he was not fighting, spent most of his time hunting and entertaining.

   _____

   _____

4. In some places, a serf wore a brass ring similar to a dog collar around his neck. Both his name and the name of his lord were inscribed on it.

   _____

   _____

5. Some lords provided their serfs with oxen. Others did not. Some serfs could pool their meager resources and buy and share an oxen. Others could not.

   _____

   _____

From Everyday Life: The Middle Ages © 2006 Good Year Books.

Name _____   Date _____

Make a Shoe Box Diorama

Make a shoe box diorama depicting a scene from everyday life on a medieval manor. You might choose to create one of the following scenes:

1. Serfs plowing and working in the fields

2. A typical castle or manor house

3. The manor itself, with its fields, buildings, and other components

Or, you may want to think of a scene to create.

Some of the materials you will need are:

1. A large shoe box

2. Construction paper

3. Markers or watercolors and paintbrush

4. Glue or paste

5. Scissors

6. Modeling clay or small figurines

On the lines below, describe the scene your diorama depicts.

_____

_____

_____

_____

_____

_____

_____

_____

Name _____ Date _____

Fill in a Venn Diagram

Fill in the Venn diagram below with facts about medieval serfs and the plantation slaves in the southern United States before the Civil War. Where the circles overlap, list features common to both.

Medieval Serfs

Both

Plantation Slaves

From Everyday Life: The Middle Ages © 2006 Good Year Books.

Name _____ Date _____

Prepare a Time Machine Journal

Imagine that you are whisked by a time machine back to eleventh-century England. You land in one of the fields on a manor owned by Lord Snootville. The first people you encounter are William and his son, Christopher. They are plowing ground to get ready for spring planting. You are horrified to see Christopher yoked like an ox and straining to pull the plow through the thick, black soil. When you later ask "why?," you are told that they are too poor to share an ox with another serf family.

After the shock of your meeting wears off, you begin to tell William and Christopher about all the wonders of the modern age. They are, of course, flabbergasted by what you tell them, and at first they believe you might be associated in some way with witchcraft. When you assure them that you are not a witch or warlock and that you are indeed from the twenty-first century, they inch closer and plead with you to tell them more.

Suppose you were limited to seven things that you could tell William and Christopher about life in the twenty-first century. What seven inventions, developments, or wonders would you relate? After careful consideration, write your choices on the lines below.

1. _____
   _____

2. _____
   _____

3. _____
   _____

4. _____
   _____

5. _____
   _____

6. _____
   _____

7. _____
   _____

From *Everyday Life: The Middle Ages* © 2006 Good Year Books.

Castle Life

Books and movies often picture life in medieval castles as pleasant and luxurious. Nothing could be farther from the truth. Castles were dark and dank affairs, built with protection in mind rather than comfort. They were cold in winter and humid in summer. What windows existed were small and covered with oiled cloth. The only light available came from candles and torches. In time of warfare, when a castle was under siege, the entire grounds within the walls were crammed with animals and humanity. Conditions were crowded, causing people's patience to wear thin and their tempers to flare. Sometimes inhabitants were forced to live like this for months, even years. Does castle life still sound dreamy?

A typical medieval castle. Many castles were surrounded by moats, which offered protection from invaders.

As previously mentioned, not all lords owned castles. But those who did built them as strong and as secure as possible. A typical castle might be built on a hill surrounded by a wall (or even two walls) 30 feet high and from 8 to 12 feet thick. At the top of the wall there were open spaces where the defenders could fire off arrows at attackers below. There were also areas where they could dump boiling water, molten lead, or boiling tar—or anything else equally as nasty and uncomfortable—on the heads of determined invaders.

Many castles and manor houses were surrounded by moats, deep ditches filled with stagnant water. A moat might measure up to 30 or 40 feet in width and about the same in depth. A drawbridge spanned the moat, after which was a heavy iron gate called a *portcullis.* In times of danger, serfs and others who lived outside the castle crossed the drawbridge into the bailey, or open courtyard of the castle. When all were safely inside, the drawbridge was pulled up by heavy chains and the portcullis lowered. Thus, it was impossible for an invader to enter the castle grounds through its main gate.

The strongest part of the castle was the keep, or donjon, a large rectangular or round tower. Depending on the size of the castle, the keep might be anywhere

From *Everyday Life: The Middle Ages* © 2006 Good Year Books.

from 30 to 100 feet high and from 25 to 100 feet wide at the base. Its base walls were about 20 feet thick, narrowing to from 7 to 14 feet as the walls rose. The keep was a fortress within a fortress, and it was here that the lord and his family resided.

In spite of the difficulty invaders had in assaulting a well-built castle, attacks did occur. The standard technique was to lay siege to the castle—that is, simply surround it for months until the people inside ran out of food and water and had to surrender. And in spite of the boiling oil and arrows that rained down on them, invaders sometimes breached the castle's defenses. They did so by using several primitive weapons characteristic of the Middle Ages. One was the catapult, a gigantic wooden machine capable of hurling large rocks against the castle's walls. Another was the battering ram, a heavy beam often several hundred feet long with a metal "ram's head" on one end. Sometimes the beam was suspended from a large wooden scaffold. At other times, it was slung from ropes or chains. Often, however, it was carried on the shoulders of hundreds of attackers, who rammed it against a gate or wall of the castle. If the ram did its job, a gap was opened in the wall large enough for the enemy to dash through. The quickest—but riskiest—tactic was to scale the walls with ladders.

Sometimes invaders even dug tunnels under the wall and moat right into the castle. They also dug tunnels supported by large wooden beams that were purposely set afire, causing the tunnel to collapse and part of the castle wall with it. They might also shoot flaming missiles over the walls to set the buildings inside afire.

While not at war or busy defending his castle or manor house, the lord devoted much time to entertaining. Each morning he was expected to attend chapel, publicly give gifts (called *alms*) to the poor, judge any disputes, and oversee the business of his estates. By mid-morning it was time for feasting. Banquets and feasts were always held in the Great Hall, where all important activities took place. The Great Hall functioned like a giant living room, bedroom, and dining room combined. It was also where all business and justice were conducted. It was heated by a large fireplace.

The main meal of the day began between 10 and 11 A.M. and usually continued for several hours. Any dinner guests were seated according to their rank and importance. The greater nobles sat at a table on a raised platform with the lord and his family. They were referred to as high table guests. Others in attendance, whom we shall call low table guests for want of a better term, sat at long tables arranged on either side of the Great Hall. These tables were no

more than long, wide boards placed on supports similar to sawhorses. Such an arrangement is how the terms *boarding* and *boardinghouse* originated.

At the lord's high table, he and his guests ate off a fine linen tablecloth and sat in high-backed chairs. They were served by pages, young boys hopeful of someday becoming knights. Wealthier lords might be served on silver; those with more modest means used wooden plates.

Diners usually ate off trenchers, thick slices of bread on which food was stacked and which served to soak up gravy and other juices. Sometimes the guests ate the trenchers when all the other food had been consumed. At other times, the empty trenchers were thrown to the numerous castle dogs that stood around sniffing and whining for handouts. Usually, however, the trenchers were collected and distributed to the poor and the beggars assembled outside the castle walls.

Detail from an eleventh-century tapestry shows a bishop blessing the food at a banquet.

Whether high table guests or other, manners were the same. Meat was cut with either a dagger or a sword and then eaten with the fingers. There were soup spoons but no forks yet, although some guests brought their own knives. When the meal was over, everyone either licked their fingers clean or wiped them on their clothes. Sometimes they used the tablecloth as a napkin. Some grander lords provided their guests with linen napkins, but that was probably the exception rather than the rule.

Bread, meat, and wine were staples of the upper-class diet. A lord's feast always included meats. Pork, beef, mutton, wild boar, venison (deer), bear, and squirrel usually topped the menu. Many kinds of fowl, including geese, ducks, pheasants, herons, swans, and peacocks might also be a part of the meal. These were roasted and served in their feathers. In addition, shellfish and salmon often appeared on the table. Meats were complemented by various pies, tarts, and puddings. Finally, a meal could also include apples, figs, nuts, jelly, and cakes with honey. Guests who left a lord's banquet hungry had no one to blame but themselves.

From *Everyday Life: The Middle Ages* © 2006 Good Year Books.

After the meal, the lord and his guests were entertained by various performers. Sometimes there were jugglers and jesters. Jesters were clowns or fools kept by some kings and lords for the sole purpose of entertainment. They wore clown-type outfits and did their best to make people laugh. Their jokes were crude and they often criticized and got by with poking fun at their masters in front of their guests (or so we are told!).

By far the most popular of the entertainers were the minstrels. They were traveling singers and musicians whose favorite instruments included lutes, bagpipes, harps, and drums. Minstrels were important for a reason other than their music: They brought news from the outside world. Often the news and stories of what was happening elsewhere were put into verse and sung. Depending on the country or area, minstrels were also called *troubadours, minnesingers, bards,* and *jongleurs.*

A lord and his lady playing a game of chess.

While entertaining or being entertained, lords and ladies wore their finest clothing. Over a linen underdress, ladies wore dresses of either brilliantly dyed wool or of rich silk and velvet, often embroidered and trimmed with fur, a sign of nobility. They completed their attire with a wimple (a veil-like head covering) and pointed shoes.

Lords decked themselves out in equally splendid fashion. Their clothes were also made of dyed wool, linen, silk, and velvet. For a grand occasion, the typical lord might dress himself in an ankle-length tunic of colored silk (to show he did not need to work), a cape, short breeches, and long stockings that reached up past his knees. His shoes were long with the toes curled up like the prow of a ship.

Lords, of course, did not entertain constantly, and they had to find other means to keep themselves amused with or without visitors. Hunting and hawking were preferred pastimes. During winter and times of siege, they played board games such as chess, checkers, dice, and backgammon. In chapter 7, "Fun and Amusements," you will read about activities outside the castle that kept gentlemen and ladies of the noble class occupied and entertained.

Name _____ Date _____

Write a Lead Paragraph for *Castle Chatter*

Suppose newspapers existed in the Middle Ages and that you are a roving reporter for the weekly *Castle Chatter*. Suppose also that you are assigned to cover a banquet at the castle of Lord Snootville.

On the lines provided, write the lead paragraph to your story. Be sure to include answers to the five "W" questions (Who? What? When? Where? and Why?) that are characteristic of a good lead paragraph. The headline has been written for you.

Castle Chatter

✦ ✦ ✦ ✦ ✦ **October 14, AD 1102** ✦ ✦ ✦ ✦ ✦

Big Bash at Lord Snootville's
Good Time Had by All

_____

_____

_____

_____

_____

_____

_____

_____

_____

_____

_____

_____

_____

_____

_____

From *Everyday Life: The Middle Ages* © 2006 Good Year Books.

Name _____ Date _____

Solve a Castle Puzzle

ACROSS

1 Meat of sheep
3 Structure that spanned a moat
7 Machine that hurled large stones
8 Strongest part of castle
11 Banquet at which a noble entertained guests
12 Singer or musician
13 Board game enjoyed by nobles

DOWN

1 Water-filled ditch around a castle
2 A clown who often performed at feasts
4 Open courtyard
5 Battering _____
6 The great _____ of a castle
9 Heavy iron gate
10 Deer meat

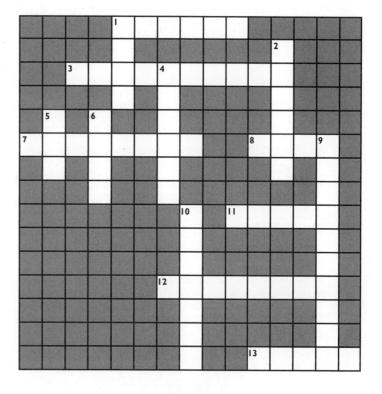

Name _____ Date _____

Help Lord Snootville Eat Better

You have read that Lord Snootville and his fellow lords did not eat what one would label "healthy" meals. They consumed far too much red meat, wine, and pastries, foods they might have limited had they known better. Their blood pressure and cholesterol levels— had there been a way of measuring these in those days—would have undoubtedly jumped right off the charts!

Help Lord Snootville to a healthier life by explaining certain things we know about good nutrition today. First, provide his lordship with answers to the following questions:

1. What is hypertension? _____
   _____

2. Why is hypertension dangerous? _____
   _____

3. How is hypertension treated? _____
   _____

4. What is cholesterol? _____
   _____

5. What is the relationship between cholesterol and good health? _____
   _____

6. How can cholesterol be maintained at safe levels?
   _____
   _____

Second, draw up a dinner menu for Lord Snootville that you think would be healthier than what he is accustomed to eating. Be sure to include only foods that were available in medieval times. Write your dinner menu on the lines below.

_____
_____
_____
_____
_____
_____
_____
_____

From Everyday Life: The Middle Ages © 2006 Good Year Books.

Name _____ Date _____

Bake a Pan of Apple Pudding

A variety of desserts was always included in meals served at the castle or manor house of a medieval lord. Among these were many kinds of puddings. Opposite is a simple recipe for apple pudding. Ask an adult to help you make a pan of this delicious treat.

Apple Pudding

1/2 cup of butter (or margarine)

2 cups of flour (plain)

2 cups of sugar

2 teaspoons of baking soda

2 eggs

1 teaspoon of cinnamon

4 cups of chopped apples

1/2 teaspoon of nutmeg

1 cup of chopped nuts*

1/4 teaspoon of allspice

*Omit nuts if you, someone in your family, or any other person who might eat a portion of your dessert is allergic to nuts.

1. Beat butter or margarine, sugar, and eggs to a cream.
2. Add chopped apples and nuts.
3. Sift together plain flour, baking soda, and the spices and add to the apple mixture.
4. Bake in a greased (butter or margarine) baking pan at 325°F for 1 hour.
5. Enjoy!

Knights and Knighthood

You might think that most young men were knights who just went through some elaborate ceremony and then dashed off on their horses to slay dragons and rescue pretty ladies in distress. It is true that early in the Middle Ages, any noble could make a person a knight and under almost any circumstance. William the Conqueror, who ruled England from 1066 to 1087, once knighted his cook for making a delicious kind of broth! Kings also knighted writers, artists, musicians, and others they saw fit to knight. However, later in the Middle Ages, as the Crusades began, men were knighted and given a religious charge: to fight in the holy wars to retake the Holy Land (Jesus' birthplace) from the Muslim Turks.

After the procedure of knighthood became more refined, a young candidate passed through several stages to become a knight. First, between the ages of seven and ten, he served a lord as a page. From ages fourteen to twenty-one, he was a squire. Then, at age twenty-one, after he had been tested and not found wanting, he became a knight. Most knights came from the upper classes, but a few ambitious peasants managed to break into the ranks of knights.

When a young boy was seven or so, he was sent away from home to the castle or manor house of a great lord to begin his training for knighthood. For seven years, his chief duty was to serve the adults, including the ladies, of the castle. He carried messages, ran errands, and waited at table during meals. The ladies of the court taught him manners and possibly how to sing and play the harp. They might also teach him how to play chess and other board games. Some pages were even taught to read and write, although literacy was not considered important to becoming a good knight.

Much of the page's time was spent outdoors. Here he boxed, wrestled, hunted, and rode with his fellow pages. He also learned to care for horses and practiced with toy swords and shields. Sometimes the miniature swords were blunt on the end. At other times, they were made of wood and therefore relatively harmless. The page's outdoor training was supervised by squires, who were known to show little pity for their young charges.

At age fourteen the page became a squire. Now his responsibilities shifted to accompanying his lord everywhere: on hunting and fishing excursions, on journeys to inspect land and other holdings, to tournaments (see chapter 9), and, of course, into battle. His primary responsibility was to care for his lord's horses and armor. He saw to it that the horses were properly exercised and groomed, and he kept his armor polished and free from rust.

From *Everyday Life: The Middle Ages* © 2006 Good Year Books.

A squire worked at mastering a variety of weapons. A stuffed dummy called the *quintain* was used for lance practice. But it was a stuffed dummy with an attitude. It was really a swiveling device with a large club at the opposite end of the dummy target. If the squire struck the target dead-center with his lance, things were fine. But if he was a little off-center, the target swung around and the club delivered a sharp blow to the back of the head. Imagine how his fellow squires must have laughed each time the lad missed the target and reaped the unpleasant consequences.

Indoors, the squire saw to his lord's every need. A lord could not even arise in the morning without his squire's assistance. The squire combed his lord's hair and helped him into his clothes. At night, he prepared his bed and helped him undress. He even took a switch or club and drove out the dogs and cats so his lord could sleep undisturbed.

Although a squire was a knight-in-training, he still had a number of duties to perform inside the house. One important job was serving his master at mealtime. Not only was he expected to serve the dishes in the correct order and manner and to carve

A squire became a knight when his lord tapped his shoulder with the flat side of a sword.

the meat properly, he had to know the right word for each type of carving. A deer was broken. A swan was lifted. A duck was unbraced. A hen got despoiled. Finally, a peacock ended up disfigured. Considering that the squire did his carving with a sword, you might make a point that every kind of meat he addressed ended up disfigured.

Although a few men were knighted on the battlefield for some brave deed—and this was often how peasants or serfs rose to knighthood—most went through an elaborate ceremony. On the day before, the young man fasted all day. He was bathed, to symbolize washing away his sins—and dressed in a white robe to symbolize service to God and purity of heart. That night, in the quiet of the church, he stood guard over his armor and prayed that he would live up to the expectations associated with knighthood.

In the morning a priest heard the young man's confession and blessed his weapons. The priest reminded him of his duties to the Church once he became a knight. Afterward, the excited squire was dressed for the ceremony. Everything he wore was cloaked in symbolism. His red tunic indicated that he was willing to shed his blood to defend the Church. His white belt or sash stood for a clean life and his white coif (cap or hat) for a pure heart. As a squire he wore spurs of silver, but as a knight he wore gold-covered spurs, which meant he was ready for service. His two-edged sword stood for self-defense and aid to others.

As the young man knelt before a noble—usually the one he had served as a squire—he was questioned about his reasons for becoming a knight. He vowed to tell the truth, to faithfully serve the king and the church, to respect women, and never to run from an enemy. His spurs were buckled on and his sword girded around his waist. This done, his lord, in a gesture referred to as the *accolade*, tapped him on each shoulder three times with a sword, declaring: "I dub thee Sir Whoever, knight." The young man was now officially a knight.

Once knighted, the new warrior was ready to do battle and perform good deeds. It was easy to distinguish a knight by his dress. He looked a little like

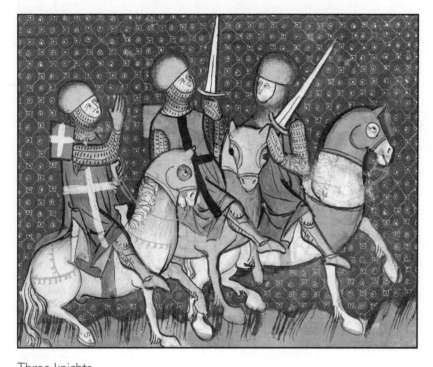

Three knights of the Middle Ages. Not only did they wear protective gear, their horses did also.

the Tin Man in *The Wizard of Oz*. By the fourteenth century, the typical knight was covered with plate armor from head to foot, some 55 pounds of it. Beneath his suit of armor he wore a hauberk, a garment made of a network of linked iron rings weighing at least another 20 pounds. Over his head he wore a steel helmet, which sometimes included a long metal nose protector. The helmet had a visor that could be raised and lowered to cover the face. Sometimes the only way for an opponent to kill a knight he had unhorsed was to raise his visor and stab him in the face. (Ouch!)

The knight's chief weapons were a lance and a sword. He used the lance in an attempt to either run an enemy through or knock him off his horse. The latter done, he resorted to his sword to finish the fight. His sword was made of fine, hammered steel, and it was the weapon he relied on most. A knight might also carry a dagger, a battle-axe, a mace, or even a flail. A mace was a nasty-looking club with a metal head, often spiked. A flail consisted of an iron ball attached to a chain, which the user swung round-and-round when engaged with an enemy.

Whether in war or peace, a knight was expected to follow a set of rules and customs. A knight's special set of rules was a code of conduct referred to as *chivalry. Chivalry* comes from the French word *chevalier,* which means "horseman" or "knight." Although at first applying only to one's skill at horsemanship, by the middle of the twelfth century, the term had taken on a whole new meaning.

The code of chivalry stressed fair play and Christian values. The knight pledged to be brave and fair in battle, to protect the weak, and to display good manners toward women. But while it is true that many knights tried their best to follow the code, just as many ignored it. It was not unusual for knights to rough up and kill serfs or to even rob an occasional church. Chivalry, therefore, was an ideal often more upheld by writers and troubadours than by the knights themselves. Regardless, in an age noted for its barbarism and instability, chivalry did play a role in transforming rough and crude medieval warriors into something resembling gentlemen.

Name _____ Date _____

Make False Statements True

All of the following statements are false. Change the words in *italics* to make them true. Write the replacement words on the lines following the statements.

1. The *accolade* was a stuffed dummy used for target practice by knights-in-training. _____

2. A noble boy served as a *squire* from the ages of seven to fourteen. _____

3. A young nobleman usually became a knight at the age of *eighteen.* _____

4. Beneath his armor, a knight wore a suit of interwoven iron rings called a *visor.* _____

5. A *mace* was a medieval weapon consisting of an iron ball attached to a chain. _____

6. A knight's *white* tunic showed that he was ready to fight to defend the Church. _____

7. A knight also wore a coif, which was a kind of *scarf.* _____

8. Knights wore *silver* spurs. _____

9. A page's chief duty was to serve the *men* of the castle or manor house. _____

10. A squire's main responsibility was to *help supervise the lord's manor.* _____

11. A page's outdoor training was supervised by *his lord.* _____

12. At a medieval dining table, meat was sliced with a *carving knife.* _____

13. *All* knights tried their best to live up to the code of chivalry. _____

14. The word "chivalry" is derived from a French word meaning *gentleman.* _____

From *Everyday Life: The Middle Ages* © 2006 Good Year Books.

Name _____ Date _____

Create a Dialogue

A young noble lad preparing to leave home to begin his training as a knight probably experienced mixed emotions. On the one hand, he was surely excited about going to live in the castle or manor house of another lord. On the other, he must have felt regret at having to leave his parents at such a tender age.

On the lines opposite, create a dialogue that might have taken place between a young knight-to-be and his parents the night before he was to depart on his great adventure.

Name _____ Date _____

Design a Coat of Arms

How did knights on the battlefield distinguish between friend and foe? After all, everyone was decked out in armor and looked pretty much the same. What prevented a knight from going after someone who was on his side?

The answer lay in *coats of arms*, identifying badges worn by knights on their armor and shields. They consisted of patterns and pictures that related to a knight's own experiences or to his family history. Look for coats of arms in a book dealing with the Middle Ages or in an encyclopedia under "heraldry."

After studying examples of coats of arms, design one of your own that you might have used had you been a knight of long ago. Use this outline of a knight's shield.

From Everyday Life: The Middle Ages © 2006 Good Year Books.

Name _____ Date _____

Contribute to a Bulletin Board Display

Create a bulletin board display centered around knights and knighthood. With a little planning, every student in class can contribute in some way to the development of the scene or scenes that become part of the project.

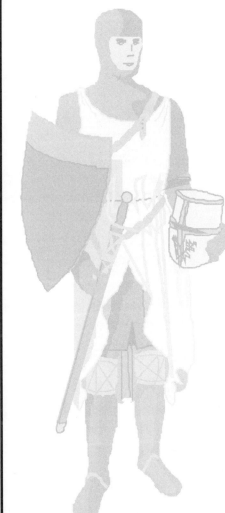

(A Teacher-directed Activity)

Some students can draw and color pictures depicting knights in various activities. Others can make sketches illustrating the armor and weapons used by knights. Still others can draw pictures of various coats of arms. Although tournaments are not covered until chapter 9, some students can make sketches of knights jousting and participating in other events associated with such medieval competition. Several more can cut out letters for the bulletin board heading, while some can measure and cut paper that will serve as the background for the display. You and your students can probably come up with even more ideas that can be illustrated and made part of the display. There should be enough to do to involve the entire class.

Materials that will prove useful are:

1. Bulletin board paper or Kraft paper
2. Markers
3. Crayons or colored pencils
4. Construction, typing, or copy paper
5. Scissors
6. Rulers
7. Glue or paste
8. Stapler and staples
9. Stencils for making letters

Legends, Myths, and Other Beliefs

If there was one thing people in the Middle Ages craved constantly, it was news—news of any kind. News of events in a distant town or district. News of what was happening just over the next hill. Even a story of some kind was welcomed. There are records of people actually stopping passing travelers and refusing to let them continue on their way until they told them a story. Whether the story was true or false mattered little. Talk about being desperate for entertainment!

You learned in chapter 3 that wandering troubadours or minstrels went from place to place "singing" the news and telling stories. Many of the stories they told were legends. Others were myths. Some were probably even "tall tales."

A legend is usually a story glorifying the deeds of some hero. It may contain some truth, but highly embellished. The legend of King Arthur, of whom more will be said later, is a classic example. Although the story relates much about sixth-century England that is factual and King Arthur apparently did exist, the cast and characters lauded in the legend never existed.

A myth is a story told to explain some event or happening in nature or the universe. Often it is a story about a god or a supernatural creature. Stories told about dragons, unicorns, vampires, and the like are myths. As with King Arthur, you'll read more about these later.

Legends and myths, along with fables (short tales designed to teach useful lessons) and tall tales (really exaggerated stories), make up part of what is called a people's *folklore*. It includes all the beliefs, stories, and customs that make one group of people separate from another. In this chapter, you will read about a few of the beliefs and stories characteristic of medieval times.

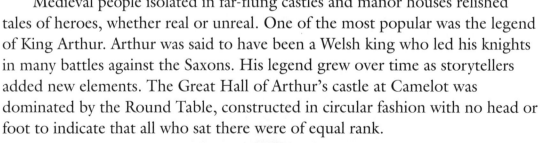

A chronicle, or book, written during the Middle Ages describes the conquests of the legendary King Arthur.

Medieval people isolated in far-flung castles and manor houses relished tales of heroes, whether real or unreal. One of the most popular was the legend of King Arthur. Arthur was said to have been a Welsh king who led his knights in many battles against the Saxons. His legend grew over time as storytellers added new elements. The Great Hall of Arthur's castle at Camelot was dominated by the Round Table, constructed in circular fashion with no head or foot to indicate that all who sat there were of equal rank.

You have probably read about some of the Knights of the Round Table. A few whose names may be familiar are Sir Lancelot, Sir Gawain, and Sir Galahad. According to the Arthurian legend, it was Sir Galahad who found the Holy Grail, the cup supposedly used by Jesus at the Last Supper. Although many searched for the magic cup, Sir Galahad was believed to have found it because he was the purest in heart.

The legend of King Arthur holds that he ruled from Camelot with his beautiful queen, Guinevere. He was assisted in his duties by Merlin, a magician. Merlin is said to have created the table around which Arthur's knights sat. Although made of marble, it had magical qualities that allowed it to be folded and carried in a coat pocket. Some people believe the Round Table was real and that it now hangs in a castle in Winchester, England.

Not every knight who sat at the Round Table was loyal to King Arthur. A few were evil and plotted against their lord. One was Sir Modred, Arthur's nephew. When Arthur was away from Camelot on a campaign, Modred led a rebellion against his uncle. Arthur returned and killed Modred, but in their struggle he himself was severely wounded. Dying, his body was placed on a barge and set adrift. The legend ends by saying that fairies then carried the body to the Isle of Avalon.

The legendary accounts of King Arthur spread from Wales through England and France and to what would later become the nations of Germany and Italy. The story was especially popular in France in the twelfth and thirteenth centuries. It was not that the French did not have their own legendary heroes to admire and sing about. They did, and one of the most famous was Roland.

In French legend, Roland was the close friend and knight of the great emperor Charlemagne. In the epic poem *The Song of Roland*, Roland fights a mighty battle against the Moors in Spain, who were Muslim invaders who conquered Spain in the eighth century. Charlemagne goes on a campaign to drive the Moors from Spain. With the help of Roland's evil stepfather, Ganelon, the Moors supposedly ambushed the rearguard of Charlemagne's army which was led by Roland in the Pyrenees Mountains. Unwilling to summon help, Roland leads his knights in a hopeless battle, killing some 100,000 of the enemy. Wounded and seeing that all is lost, Roland blows his horn to summon Charlemagne to avenge their deaths, blowing so hard that his temples burst, killing him. Roland's heroics spread to Italy, where he became known as Orlando.

Such fanciful tales of bold deeds kept people entertained during the Middle Ages. In addition to keeping up with the latest in legends, medieval Europeans had a host of supernatural beings and animals to sort out. These included giants, goblins, trolls, witches, werewolves, vampires, dragons, and unicorns. Of these, dragons and unicorns are the two most closely identified with the Middle Ages.

Everyone in the Middle Ages who claimed to have seen a dragon generally agreed on its appearance. It was snakelike and had wings like a bat or a bird. Its body was covered with scales like a reptile, and it had claws like an eagle. Finally, it had a long, alligator-like tail that could inflict considerable pain on anyone unlucky enough to come into contact with it. Some dragons breathed fire, which added a further dimension to their already terrible qualities.

This painting shows one version of what medieval people thought a dragon might look like.

How people came to believe in dragons is at best a guess. One person's guess is as valid as another's. Dragon myths long preceded the Middle Ages, existing in ancient Egypt, Greece, Rome, the Middle East, and China. In medieval Christianity, the dragon became a symbol of evil and paganism (not believing in the Christian God). The Normans who invaded England in 1066 used the dragon as a symbol of war. Dragons, like all the other mythical beings of the time, probably sprang from superstitions associated with people desperately trying to explain the mysteries of the world in which they lived.

If you look through a book on the Middle Ages, you will probably see the images of unicorns on shields and tapestries. Shields, of course, were devices used by knights to ward off blows in combat. Tapestries are elaborate scenes woven in fabric, an art form for which the Middle Ages are famous. Tapestries were often used in the Middle Ages to cover the dank walls of castles and manor houses.

Pictures of unicorns show a horse-like animal with a horn protruding out of its forehead. The unicorn's horn was the source of its strength and power. Paintings from the time show animals gathered around a pond or stream with a

From *Everyday Life: The Middle Ages* © 2006 Good Year Books.

unicorn in the midst, stirring the water with its horn. It was a common belief that poisoned water could be made pure from contact with the horn of the unicorn. Therefore, cups supposedly made from a unicorn's horn (most often rhinoceros) were in high demand among the nobility, who thought such a cup would protect them from poisoning. The unicorn also was a common symbol of Christ in medieval art and literature.

Along with all the legendary heroes and mythical creatures was an endless list of superstitions. People went about wearing a variety of stones, herbs, rings, and magic charms in the belief that such objects fended off devils and brought good luck. (Some people still do today.) Philters, or magic potions, were available for almost every purpose, either to attract or turn away the love of another. Sometimes magic potions were not even needed; some extraordinary and distasteful act might accomplish the desired purpose. One common belief, for example, was that a woman could prevent conception by spitting three times into the mouth of a frog!

Superstition even spilled over into law. You may have read about trial by combat and trial by ordeal. These were two procedures used in the Middle Ages to appeal a judgment of guilt against one. Here is how they worked.

In trial by combat, the accused and his accuser squared off on the field of battle. If the accused emerged victorious or succeeded in defending himself till nightfall, he was declared innocent. If he was defeated, then he was judged guilty. It couldn't get any simpler than that, could it?

A painting depicting a unicorn. The unicorn was believed to be a horse-like animal with a horn.

Trial by ordeal was almost as uncomplicated. The accused was put through some unpleasant experience designed to prove his guilt or innocence. He or she might have to carry a piece of hot iron in one hand (a common ordeal for women), or walk barefoot through a fire, or stick an arm into a pot of boiling water to retrieve a stone. If the wounds did not become infected and if they healed quickly, the person was judged innocent. If, as was undoubtedly true in most cases, the opposite resulted, then the person was found guilty and had to pay the consequences.

These were but some of the beliefs that influenced the lives and behavior of people in the Middle Ages. You can find many more by consulting some of the books in your school library.

Name _____ Date _____

Use Context Clues to Complete Sentences

Fill in the sentences on the page with the words from the word box.

added
backward
based
beliefs
collection
continued
Earth
elsewhere
exception
glorify
important
invented
latter
shores
tales
understand

Folklore is an _____ part of the history and culture of all nations. Since ancient times, people have _____ heroes and mythical beings either to _____ their own achievements or to explain things they did not _____.

America is no _____. A distinct folklore of characters and beliefs began with Native Americans and _____ with Europeans and others who later came to these _____. And these characters and beliefs are every bit as fanciful and appealing as those created by people _____.

Take the Native Americans, for example. They invented stories to explain everything from how the _____ was created to how humankind got fire. The colonists followed and _____ their tales and superstitions to the list. For example, the stories of Evangeline or the Angel of Hadley are both _____ in part on truth. And, later, what about the likes of Paul Bunyan, John Henry, and Pecos Bill? Or such tall _____ as the Hoop Snake or the Gillygaloo, the _____ a funny-looking bird that laid square eggs? Or the Goofus Bird, which was said to fly _____ because it didn't care where it was going?

Every section of America has its _____ of legendary heroes, mythical creatures, and tall tales and yarns. Together with the _____ of other regions, they form a folklore rich in color and imagination.

From Everyday Life: The Middle Ages © 2006 Good Year Books.

Name _____ Date _____

Make a Cereal Box Report

From the information presented in the chapter, prepare a cereal box report on a legendary or mythical character associated with the Middle Ages. Or, if you prefer, find and read about others in an encyclopedia or in any book dealing with the Middle Ages or mythology and choose one of these for your report.

Here Is What You Will Need:

1. An empty cereal box, or any similar box

2. White paper, either typing or printer paper preferable

3. Glue or paste

4. A felt-tipped pen, or any pen suitable for drawing

5. Scissors

Here Is What You Do:

1. Glue or paste white paper over all sides of the box.

2. On the top edge of the box, write the name of the legendary or mythical character you have researched.

3. On one side panel, write the category your selection falls under (legendary hero, mythical creature, etc.).

4. On the other side panel, write which country or countries your selection is most associated with.

5. On the front of the box, draw a picture of your hero or mythical creature.

6. On the back, if the topic of your report is a legendary hero, write a brief account of his or her exploits. If you are reporting on some mythical creature, describe its appearance and list its magical powers or characteristics.

Name _____ Date _____

Name Those Synonyms and Antonyms

A synonym is a word that has the same meaning as another word. An antonym is a word opposite in meaning to another word.

Below is a list of twenty words taken from the chapter. Write a synonym and an antonym for each. You may use a thesaurus or dictionary if necessary.

	Synonym	**Antonym**
1. craved (v)	_____	_____
2. distant (adj)	_____	_____
3. glorifying (v)	_____	_____
4. laud (v)	_____	_____
5. relished (v)	_____	_____
6. loyal (adj)	_____	_____
7. popular (adj)	_____	_____
8. admire (v)	_____	_____
9. summon (v)	_____	_____
10. bold (adj)	_____	_____
11. considerable (adj)	_____	_____
12. valid (adj)	_____	_____
13. often (adv)	_____	_____
14. almost (adv)	_____	_____
15. attract (v)	_____	_____
16. extraordinary (adj)	_____	_____
17. distasteful (adj)	_____	_____
18. exaggerated (v)	_____	_____
19. include (v)	_____	_____
20. real (adj)	_____	_____

From Everyday Life: The Middle Ages © 2006 Good Year Books.

Name _____ Date _____

Conduct a Superstition Survey

It is easy for us today to look back on people in the Middle Ages and laugh at their superstitions. "How dumb!" we might think. "How could intelligent people have believed such nonsense?" we might say.

Before we congratulate ourselves on being so advanced and sophisticated, we should stop and consider the many superstitions and "old wives' tales" that are still widespread today. Some of these may have a profound effect on the daily activities of people we know. Maybe you yourself do or do not do certain things because of a superstitious belief.

With this in mind, ask your parent(s), grandparent(s), guardian, or friends to help you make a list of four superstitious beliefs they know that are still prevalent today. On the lines below, identify each superstition and write your opinion as well. Tell how you think each superstition might have originated or whether it has any basis for truth.

1. Superstition #1 _____

   _____

   My opinion: _____

   _____

2. Superstition #2 _____

   _____

   My opinion: _____

   _____

3. Superstition #3 _____

   _____

   My opinion: _____

   _____

4. Superstition #4 _____

   _____

   My opinion: _____

   _____

From Everyday Life: The Middle Ages © 2006 Good Year Books.

The Medieval Church

The Middle Ages were a time of superstition and uncertainty—a time when people tried to cope with the mysteries and dangers that dominated their everyday lives. Work was hard, life expectancy was short, and the future held little hope for anything better. Many people believed that the end of the world was near, and, as a result, merely tried to endure until the appointed time came. This fatalistic attitude was especially prominent during the Dark Ages, as the early part of the Middle Ages is often called. The time agreed upon by most for the world's end was the year 1000.

These ruins are all that is left of this Irish church and churchyard from the Middle Ages.

Under such conditions, it is not surprising that people turned to the Church for guidance and comfort. But what is meant here by "the Church"? Until the eleventh century there was one church in medieval Europe. That church was the Catholic Church. The word *catholic* means "universal," indicating that it was the only church in existence at the time. In the fifth century, the head of the Church, the Bishop of Rome, assumed the title of pope. In the Latin language, *pope* means "father."

Differences in beliefs and control led the Catholic Church to split into two distinct churches in 1054. The church in the region of the old western Roman Empire came to be known as the Roman Catholic Church. Its was centered at Rome and its head was the pope. The church in the eastern half of the Roman Empire, a part that survived until the fifteenth century, became the Greek Orthodox Church. It was centered at Constantinople, a city that is today called Istanbul. Its head was the patriarch of Constantinople.

Now back to the medieval Christian Church in western Europe before 1054. In power and prestige, its hold on members was absolute and complete. People were born into the Church and remained under its authority until their deaths. The Church recorded their births, conducted their marriage ceremonies, christened their children, and officiated at their deaths. It often cared for them

From *Everyday Life: The Middle Ages* © 2006 Good Year Books.

if they were poor, sick, aged, or orphaned. The Middle Ages was also the time when many men and women entered monasteries and convents, either to escape the world or because they had no other means of support. Because the Church's influence in people's lives was so far-reaching, the devout were careful not to raise the displeasure of the clergy (church officials) in any way.

So what happened if someone came into conflict with the Church? What could the Church do? The answer to that question is "plenty." The Church had the power to excommunicate any person who violated church law. Excommunication was the act of cutting off someone from all religious services and privileges. This meant that he or she could not receive any of the sacraments, important ceremonies that included baptism, marriage, and the last rites administered to a dying person. In short, an excommunicated person was no longer a member of the Church. In a time when heaven and hell were unquestioned, this was a terrible fate.

Sometimes excommunication was applied to an entire region or nation. In such cases, it was referred to as an interdict. This happened when a ruler came into conflict with church authorities in Rome. Perhaps an argument arose concerning land. Or perhaps it had to do with the appointment of a bishop in the ruler's domain. Whatever the reason, the pope would close all of the churches in that country until the rebellious ruler knuckled under. Until he did, all his subjects were thought to be in danger of eternal damnation.

The power of the medieval Church can best be demonstrated in the story of Henry IV. Henry was emperor of the Holy Roman Empire, a loose-knit group of kingdoms and states that was neither holy, Roman, nor really an empire. The empire included what is today Germany and all or parts of western and central Europe. It was never a powerful or an influential force in European politics, and it is mentioned here only because it was the focal point of a tremendous struggle between the pope and a medieval ruler.

In 1069, a few years after Henry IV began to rule the Holy Roman Empire, he came into conflict with the pope, Gregory VII. Their argument stemmed from the appointment of important church officials throughout Henry's realm. Henry claimed it was his right to appoint bishops and the like. Gregory countered that this was solely a power of the Church. When the argument continued, Gregory excommunicated the defiant emperor. At the same time, he informed Henry's subjects that they were relieved of any further allegiance to their ruler. Now Henry had a real problem: Some of his nobles rose up in revolt against his leadership.

Henry IV knew he could not win his battle with Gregory VII. When even the serfs and townspeople turned against him, he made his way quickly to Italy to make things right. There, at a castle high in the Apennine Mountains where the pope was staying, Henry was forced to stand outside barefoot in the snow for three days before Gregory agreed to see him. When at last he was admitted, he knelt before the pope and asked his forgiveness.

Holy Roman Emperor Henry IV was forced to ask Pope Gregory for forgiveness after defying him and trying to take some of his power.

Often the Church used its immense powers to maintain law and order. Two Church decrees were designed to this end. One was the Peace of God. It forbade fighting around certain places—such as churches and monasteries—and promised excommunication for anyone who killed a noncombatant (civilian) during battle. Another was the Truce of God. It forbade lords and knights to engage in combat from Wednesday evening to Monday morning, as well as on special holidays. As time went on, more exempt days were added until war was permitted on only about 80 days of the year.

Did medieval lords and knights obey these church decrees? Some did, others did not. Some not only fought in the vicinity of churches and monasteries but robbed them in the process. Private wars between rival feudal lords and their armies continued until kings became strong enough to bring them under control. But this did not begin to occur until well into the thirteenth century.

The medieval Church did more than care for the unfortunate and try to keep private wars at a minimum. One of its most important contributions was saving the writings of the ancient Greeks and Romans from destruction in the wake of the fall of the Roman Empire. This preservation of ancient knowledge and culture was the work of the monasteries of western Europe.

Monasteries grew from groups of hermits who banded together and became monks. Hermits were men who went off into the wilderness or the desert to live by themselves. Some did so hoping to rid their lives of sin. Others became hermits simply to be alone. The word *monk*, in fact, is derived from a

From *Everyday Life: The Middle Ages* © 2006 Good Year Books.

Greek word meaning "alone." It was such men who worked together in the monasteries copying and illuminating manuscripts, or books, by hand.

To illuminate a manuscript meant to embellish it with colorful pictures and designs. Usually the first letter of a page or chapter heading in a book was vastly enlarged and decorated. Within its borders, monks drew designs of many objects: birds, vines, insects, flowers, and the like. Both the background of the letters and the designs sketched within it were illustrated in bright colors. Monks also illustrated the margins of individual manuscript pages in the same manner.

Although illuminated manuscripts were considered works of art, their real importance lay elsewhere. In an age before the invention of the printing press, monks sat for hours at their desks painstakingly copying books by hand. They not only copied and therefore preserved old manuscripts written in Latin and Greek; they also made copies of the Bible as well. A monk might devote well over a year to making and illustrating a copy of the Bible.

Monks contributed to medieval society in still other ways. They ran schools, provided guest houses for travelers, and helped spread Christianity among pagan peoples. They even influenced farming methods of the day, teaching the serfs the importance of letting one field lie fallow each year to preserve its fertility. Their fields, gardens, and orchards served as models that were much imitated throughout Europe.

Colorful drawings in illuminated manuscripts highlighted capital letters.

In a time when national governments were weak and largely ineffective, the medieval Church did its best to maintain an orderly society and look out after the needs of its members. Its importance in medieval life cannot be overemphasized.

Name _____ Date _____

Draw Conclusions from What You Have Read

The ability to draw conclusions is an important skill. Can you read a paragraph, think about the facts presented, and form an opinion based on those facts?

Try your hand at the following situations. Then, on the lines provided, write your answers to the questions connected with each.

1. St. Simeon Stylites might have been the champion hermit of all time. In the fifth century, he built a pillar, or column, 50 feet high. On top of the pillar, he constructed a platform wide enough to stand and sit but not to lie down. For 36 years, he remained atop his perch. He never came down, regardless of the weather. His friends brought him food and water by climbing a ladder to the top.

What do you think St. Simeon Stylites was trying to prove?

_____

_____

2. The Vikings who invaded Europe in the ninth century eventually converted to Christianity. But suppose the Vikings had clung to their pagan beliefs and simply destroyed all of the Christian churches and monasteries of western Europe.

What might have happened to learning and culture had the above scenario taken place?

_____

_____

3. Let's look at a hypothetical situation involving Lord Snootville, whom you met in a previous chapter. Suppose Lord Snootville is planning a sneak attack on the lord just down the road—his archenemy, Lord Nuisance. Although it is Thursday, Snootville decides to carry out his attack the following morning.

Hearing of his plans, Snootville's wife pleads with him to wait until Monday. Why is she so desperate in imploring her husband not to do battle over the weekend?

_____

_____

From Everyday Life: The Middle Ages © 2006 Good Year Books.

Name _____ Date _____

Solve Some Cathedral Math

During the Middle Ages, towns competed in building the most imposing Gothic cathedrals. (*Gothic* was a term used by later scholars who thought that the classic architecture of the Greeks and Romans had been corrupted by the invading Goths who overran the Roman Empire.) When one town completed a cathedral with a particularly high vault, or ceiling, others were determined to surpass it.

To the right are figures showing the heights of vaults of the cathedrals of four medieval French towns. Use the information listed and the spaces provided to work the problems at the bottom.

French City	Height of Cathedral Vault
Paris	114 feet
Chartres	118 feet
Rheims	124 feet
Amiens	138 feet

1. What was the average height of the vaults of the four cathedrals? _____ feet

2. The vault of the Amiens cathedral was 24 feet, or _____ %, higher than the vault of the cathedral in Paris.

3. If one foot equals 0.3048 meters, how many meters tall was the vault of each of the cathedrals? Round your answers to the nearest whole meter.

Paris _____ meters
Chartres _____ meters
Rheims _____ meters
Amiens _____ meters

Name _____   Date _____

Create an Illuminated Letter

In the space below, draw a large capital letter that might have represented the first letter on a page from an illuminated manuscript of the Middle Ages.

Within the borders of the letter, draw tiny pictures of your choice. You may either draw some of the objects mentioned in the narrative or think of others yourself. Use bright colors to illuminate both the letter and the objects you sketch within it. You can find examples of illuminated letters by looking in such sources as a book on the Middle Ages or an encyclopedia.

From Everyday Life: The Middle Ages © 2006 Good Year Books.

Name _____ Date _____

Recall Information You Have Read

Remember that the ability to recall information is an important learning skill—a skill that grows in importance from one grade level to the next. Without looking back over the chapter, define or identify as best you can the names and terms listed here.

1. Dark Ages
_____
_____

2. catholic
_____
_____

3. Greek Orthodox Church
_____
_____

4. sacraments
_____
_____

5. excommunication
_____
_____

6. interdict
_____
_____

7. Peace of God
_____
_____

8. Truce of God
_____
_____

9. hermit
_____
_____

10. illuminated manuscript
_____
_____

Fun and Amusements

Medieval life was not all doom and gloom. Even in the feudal age, when constant warfare made life uncertain, people had their moments of fun. As the Middle Ages progressed and society became more orderly, other opportunities for entertainment and recreation arose.

You learned in chapter 2 that the serfs looked forward to Sundays and feast days to engage in such recreational activities as football and dancing. But what about the nobles? How did they keep themselves entertained between bouts of fighting?

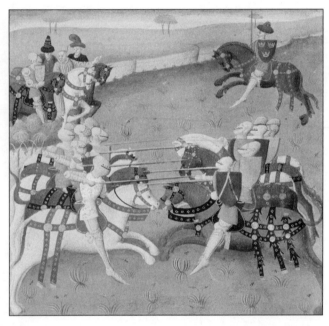

Knights jousting at a tournament during the Middle Ages.

One form of recreation that always comes to mind with regard to knights is the tournament. Today we use the word *tournament* to refer to any contest in which competitors play a series of games. It might pertain to such sports as basketball, golf, or bowling. Or it might involve activities such as chess or debate. In medieval times, it always referred to groups of mounted knights armed with blunted (usually) weapons who engaged in contests for prizes and honor.

Richard Armour, one of America's best-known humor writers of the 1950s, described tournaments as contests "where knights were horsed, unhorsed, or just 'horsing' around." Although joking, Armour wasn't far from the truth. Strange things happened at these highly popular contests. This was especially true in early tournaments where a free-for-all called the *melee* or *tourney* took center stage.

In the melee, two teams of knights faced off in an open field. The goal of each team was to knock as many of its opponents from their horses as possible and capture them. Although the object was to capture—not kill—one's opponents, the contest was nearly as bloody and violent as a real battle. Until rules to limit injury were instituted in the fourteenth century, the teams would go at each other as if in real combat, using actual weapons. In one melee in Cologne, Germany, some sixty knights were killed during a daylong contest. One can only wonder at the death toll had the knights not been "playing"!

From *Everyday Life: The Middle Ages* © 2006 Good Year Books.

In fact, so many knights were killed or maimed that the pope and King Henry II of England banned tournaments for a period in the thirteenth century.

Often a melee ranged over an entire countryside. In the process, good farmland and orchards were trampled underfoot. One mock battle that involved three thousand knights tore up acres of valuable vineyards in France. Participating knights, however, cared little for the damage they caused. Their only concern was with the wealth that could be attained from unhorsing another knight. Any knight knocked from his horse by an opposing knight's lance had to surrender his horse, his armor, and his weapons to the victor. In addition, the defeated knight was often carried off and held for ransom. Some game!

In time, tournaments became more civil, and the melee was replaced by the *joust* between individual knights. Again, the purpose was to knock the opponent off his horse. Rules of fair play required a knight to aim his lance above the waist and strike his adversary's shield. A blow that landed otherwise was considered unsportsmanlike and drew hisses from the crowd.

The joust was surrounded by all the excitement and fanfare of a modern sporting event. Nobles and their ladies wore their finest clothes and sat in stands draped with pennants and coats of arms. Musicians blared away before each contest and often accented a particularly fine stroke by a contestant with a congratulatory blast. (Sounds like the movies, doesn't it?) The multiday spectacle included dances, feasts, and music, for the particular enjoyment of the ladies. Unfortunately, the local commoners were often made to house the combatants—who typically were better fighting than at paying their bills.

Many knights, called *knights-errant*, earned their livelihood traveling from tournament to tournament. Although a victor might be rewarded with a prize, the real prize lay in gaining possession of a defeated opponent's horse and armor. Thus, tournaments were good ways for a knight with limited financial or social prospects to earn a living, and if he was lucky, come to the attention of a great noble who might make him a vassal. When tournaments were banned, knights-errant complained that such legal action deprived them of a way to earn a living.

Tournaments in some form remained in existence until the seventeenth century. By that time, however, contests were limited to tilting. Tilting was similar to jousting, except that a wooden rail called a *tilt* separated the jousters along the length of the course. Contestants could still charge at each other at top speed, but the rail kept their horses from colliding. In this way, tilting was a more humane sport than jousting.

When not participating in or watching tournaments, nobles kept themselves occupied by hunting. A popular form of hunting was falconry. This involved hunting birds and small animals with a trained falcon, or hawk. Noblewomen as well as noblemen enjoyed the sport. Some ladies, in fact, found it fashionable to go about with a chained falcon on their wrists even when not hunting. Sometimes they attended church with the birds perched on their arms.

A falconer with his falcon. Noble men and ladies used falcons for hunting.

A well-trained falcon was highly prized. On the hunt, it was taught to sit quietly on its owner's gloved wrist with its head covered by a leather hood. The hood was designed to keep the falcon calm until its services were needed. When some game bird or small animal was spotted, the falcon's hood was removed and it flew off in hot pursuit. After catching its prey, the falcon was trained to fly back onto the wrist of its owner, who then replaced its hood.

Common people, of course, could not engage in such pastimes as jousting or falconry. But they could enjoy the many activities associated with fairs. When a fair opened outside the walls of a castle or a monastery (and later within the limits of a town), everyone was free to attend. Even pickpockets regarded fairs as annual events staged for their benefit.

A fair was an event at which traveling merchants met to sell their goods. In the years when towns were few and travel was dangerous, fairs were sponsored by feudal lords and church officials. Merchants set up their booths or stalls outside the walls of castles and monasteries and displayed their wares for interested buyers to see. Sometimes the lords and monks even supplied the stalls themselves. In return for the protection they afforded the merchants, they received a tax on all goods sold.

Like their modern-day namesakes, medieval fairs offered something for everyone. Their main feature, of course, was the wide variety of goods for sale. There was fine woolen cloth from England and Flanders. There were daggers and swords from Germany and copper pots from Belgium. From Spain came soft leather gloves and slippers, while Alsace, a region of France, offered tubs,

From *Everyday Life: The Middle Ages* © 2006 Good Year Books.

for which it was famous. In addition, shoppers and browsers could look over other items ranging from brooches and hats to saddles and carts.

The most prized goods on display at fairs were hard-to-get luxuries from the East. These included spices, silks, rugs, perfumes, and jewels. Spices were especially valued for preserving and adding flavor to meats and other foods. Usually only the nobles could afford to buy such items, but it mattered little to the common people. They occupied themselves enjoying the many other attractions fairs had to offer.

Many people were drawn to fairs simply to mingle and to talk. As you have learned in a previous chapter, news was hard to come by in the Middle Ages. Fairs afforded people the opportunity to find out what was happening elsewhere in the world. They shared stories and swapped yarns and gossip. Just talking to someone outside their own town or region was entertainment enough for some fairgoers.

Others were attracted by the excitement and the numerous performers on hand. There were musicians, actors, jugglers, acrobats, and tightrope walkers, all to be enjoyed for only a few pennies. There were also trained animal acts, horse races, and other activities. Fairs were probably as exciting to the people of medieval Europe as they are to us today.

After travel became less dangerous, the sites of fairs shifted from castles and monasteries to towns. Often these fairs were held around the time of a religious pilgrimage, which brought additional prospective customers to town. The towns of the Champagne region of France became famous for its trade shows. Six fairs lasting six weeks each were held each year, which meant that a large fair was always taking place somewhere in Europe. At each fair, the streets of the town were decorated with flowers and colored paper, and at night flaming torches lighted the way. Lively parties were always going on in the town's popular inns.

As you can see, events such as tournaments and fairs provided much-needed entertainment and amusement in an age noted for its hardships.

A scene from a medieval fair, with various craftsmen showing their wares.

Name _____ Date _____

Make a Collage

Have you ever made a collage? A collage is a picture made by pasting items such as parts of pictures or other materials to a background. The background can be a piece of cardboard, wood, or canvas. What you attach to the background to illustrate your theme is up to you.

For ideas, look through magazines and newspapers for illustrations that could be worked into a fair collage. Look for pictures of animal exhibits, arts and crafts, cooking exhibits, games, and all the rides that young people find so thrilling: the roller coaster, the Ferris wheel, bumper cars, and a host of others.

In chapter 7 you read about the excitement connected with medieval fairs: the exhibits of goods, the various kinds of entertainment, and the general gaiety that characterized such events. The county and state fairs that we enjoy so much today grew out of those exhibitions held during the Middle Ages.

With these facts in mind, make a collage depicting some of the activities associated with modern-day fairs. Cut out appropriate pictures and photographs of magazines and newspapers (or draw your own) and glue them on your background. If you have ticket stubs or any small souvenirs or keepsakes from a recent visit, attach them along with your pictures. Anything associated with the theme of your collage is acceptable.

To get a better idea of how to arrange cutouts and other materials on your background, it might prove helpful to study pictures of collages before you begin.

Here are some materials that will prove useful in preparing your collage:

1. A large piece of cardboard or some other material to use as your background

2. Glue or paste

3. Construction paper or some other kind of paper suitable for drawing

4. Felt-tipped pens, crayons, or colored pencils

5. Scissors

6. Illustrations and pictures cut from magazines and newspapers

From *Everyday Life: The Middle Ages* © 2006 Good Year Books.

Name _____ Date _____

Write a Descriptive Account

How skilled are you at describing things you have seen? Could you watch an event such as an athletic contest or a play and describe it in a report that would be both informative and entertaining?

Try your hand at writing a descriptive account of a joust between Sir Bold and Sir Stouthearted, medieval England's bravest and most popular knights. Through a time machine, you have been whisked back to Merry Ol' England and deposited in the stands at a tournament next to none other than Lord Snootville and his charming wife, Vaina, both of whom eagerly await the contest between the distinguished knights.

Now write your descriptive account. Continue on a separate sheet of paper if necessary.

From Everyday Life: The Middle Ages © 2006 Good Year Books.

Name _____ Date _____

Compare Entertainment Then and Now

On the lines provided, list ways in which two popular kinds of entertainment in the Middle Ages—tournaments and fairs—were both alike and different from similar forms of amusement today.

Medieval Tournaments/Modern Sporting Events

Similarities

1. _____

2. _____

3. _____

Differences

1. _____

2. _____

3. _____

Medieval Fairs/Modern Fairs

Similarities

1. _____

2. _____

3. _____

Differences

1. _____

2. _____

3. _____

From *Everyday Life: The Middle Ages* © 2006 Good Year Books.

Name _____ Date _____

Complete a Vocabulary Exercise

Select the meaning of each word as it is used in chapter 7. Write the letter of the correct meaning on the line at the left. The paragraph in which each word appears in the narrative is written in parentheses.

_____ 1. **contest** (paragraph 3)

(a) trial of skill (b) argue against (c) dispute

_____ 2. **mounted** (paragraph 3)

(a) fixed in a setting or backing (b) on a horse
(c) in a position for use

_____ 3. **goal** (paragraph 5)

(a) aim or desire
(b) place in a game where points are scored
(c) a score in an athletic contest

_____ 4. **mock** (paragraph 6)

(a) ridicule (b) not real (c) disregard

_____ 5. **rail** (paragraph 10)

(a) complain bitterly (b) a kind of bird
(c) part of a fence

_____ 6. **occupied** (paragraph 11)

(a) busy (b) filled (c) took possession of

_____ 7. **stall** (paragraph 14)

(a) become stuck in mud, snow, etc.
(b) to delay or play for time
(c) a small, enclosed place where goods are sold

_____ 8. **main** (paragraph 15)

(a) most important (b) a large pipe
(c) the open sea

_____ 9. **drawn** (paragraph 17)

(a) hauled (b) strained (c) attracted

_____ 10. **afforded** (paragraph 17)

(a) had the money for (b) provided (c) yielded

The Crusades

Around 1092 startling news arrived from the Holy Land. Religious pilgrims making journeys to Jerusalem, the birthplace of Jesus, were not allowed to enter the city, and they were being mistreated and sometimes killed, by the Muslim Turks who had taken over the area in 1071. Invading Turks had conquered much of the Byzantine Empire, and Emperor Alexius sent a plea for help to his fellow Christians in the West.

Pope Urban II responded by calling a church council, or meeting, at Clermont in France early in 1095. He preached to the crowd about the dangers of the "infidel" Turks. Not only had they conquered Jerusalem, but they were threatening Constantinople as well. Urban II called for a crusade, or "holy war," to recover the Holy Land (Palestine). He announced that a crusade would set out that very summer.

In this detail from an eleventh-century manuscript, Peter the Hermit is shown urging Christians to retake the Holy Land from the Muslims.

One of those roused to action was Peter the Hermit, who apparently had recently returned from Jerusalem. He rode through the streets of French towns on a mule, preaching at the top of his voice about the dastardly deeds of the Turks and urging everyone in the crowds to join in a crusade. Apparently he made quite an impression; although his hair and clothes were disheveled, he developed a reputation for holiness. People even plucked hairs from his mule's tail to keep as religious relics.

Peter the Hermit recruited fifteen thousand commoners and peasants and later met up with another group led by a poor knight called Walter the Penniless. They left France and Germany for the Holy Land in May 1096. Their combined groups contained only a handful of trained knights. Many of the crusaders were women and children traveling along with their husbands and fathers.

Few among Peter and Walter's motley army had the slightest idea where they were going. They also had no discipline and generally made themselves unpopular by looting and pillaging in eastern Europe along the journey. It is

From *Everyday Life: The Middle Ages* © 2006 GoodYear Books.

not surprising that this ill-advised crusade, known as the *People's* or *Peasant's Crusade,* failed. Most of its participants either died of disease along the way or were killed by the Turks upon reaching their destination.

The first real crusade set out a few months later. Led by French nobles, it succeeded in temporarily wresting Jerusalem from Turkish control. The Turks, however, recaptured the city after a short interval. What followed was almost 200 years of war that lasted off and on from 1095 to 1291. Although the Crusaders never permanently held the Holy Land, they did succeed in gaining safe passage for Christians making pilgrimages.

Perhaps the most remembered of the crusades was the third. Called the "Crusade of the Three Kings," it was led by Richard "the Lion-Hearted" of England, Philip Augustus of France, and Frederick Barbarossa of the Holy Roman Empire. This unsuccessful venture bordered on being a comedy of errors. Frederick Barbarossa fell and drowned trying to swim in a stream in Syria. Afterward, Richard and Philip argued over leadership of their combined armies. Philip grew weary of the whole thing and took his army home to France, where he fought English forces that had earlier seized territory there. Richard failed to capture Jerusalem and on his way home was captured and held for ransom by Frederick's son, Henry IV. So ended the famous Third Crusade.

Why did Europeans drop everything they were doing and go on crusades? The reasons are many. Most went out of religious fervor and a sincere desire to free the Holy Land from Turkish control. The stories they heard of atrocities committed against Christian pilgrims spurred them to action. They considered the Turks infidels, or disbelievers, who deserved to be dealt with in the harshest terms. Before leaving for the Holy Land, crusaders sewed a cross on their garments. It is from *crux,* the Latin word for cross, that the words *crusade* and *crusader* are derived.

For every person motivated to join a crusade out of religious zeal, there was probably one who went solely for personal reasons. Many knights saw a chance to win fame, wealth, and land. Debtors volunteered when told their debts would be erased. Criminals joined in exchange for having their punishments commuted. Serfs left their fields upon being promised their freedom if they fought the Turks. And all who went were assured immediate entry into heaven if they were killed in battle.

Even children heeded the call. In 1212 there were two disastrous Children's Crusades. One was led by a French shepherd boy named Stephen. The other left Cologne in what is now Germany under the leadership of a lad named Nicholas.

One day while tending his sheep in the fields, Stephen claimed that he had a vision in which Jesus directed him to lead a crusade to the Holy Land. While adults smirked, Stephen enlisted some thirty thousand young people whose average age was about twelve and prepared to set out. No amount of pleading on the part of frantic parents could convince their children not to go.

Stephen and his army departed with no weapons. They believed faith and love alone would see them to victory. They also believed that when they reached Marseilles on the Mediterranean coast that the sea would part and allow them to cross. After all, this had happened with the Israelites long ago when the Red Sea parted and allowed them to leave Egypt. Surely a similar miracle would happen and allow the children simply to walk across to the Holy Land.

The Mediterranean Sea, of course, did not part. But all was not lost, or at least the children thought. Sailors at the port offered to ferry them across at no charge. The sailors said they would do this just for the love of the Lord. Singing hymns, the children crammed into seven boats and looked forward to continuing their journey.

Unfortunately for Stephen's group, the sailors who appeared so kind turned out to be pirates. Their intention was to take the children to north Africa and sell them as slaves. Two of the seven pirate boats wrecked off the coast of Sardinia, a large island south of Italy, but the other five arrived safely in Tunisia. There the doomed children were sold into slavery and were never heard from again.

The shepherd boy Stephen leading his army of children on their ill-fated crusade to the Holy Land.

In Germany, young Nicholas too believed that God had chosen him to lead a crusade. Unmoved by the jeers and scoffs of those around him, he gathered together some twenty thousand children and departed. Neither he nor his followers could imagine the horrors that lay ahead for them—horrors much worst than those encountered by Stephen's group.

From *Everyday Life: The Middle Ages* © 2006 GoodYear Books.

At first all went well for Nicholas and his band. They traveled without incident down the Rhine River, picking up additional recruits along the way. Then disaster struck. High in the Alps, thousands of children died of hunger and exposure. When the survivors of Nicholas's army reached Italy, they split into several groups. One made it to Rome, where Pope Innocent III released them from their crusade vows, saying they were too young. What happened to the children is unclear. Some turned back and were killed on the way home. Others succeeded in reaching home safely. Some apparently stayed in Italy, but many were probably sold, like Stephen's group, into slavery in the east.

This twelfth-century sculpture shows a returning crusader being greeted by his wife.

The Crusades continued at intervals until almost the end of the thirteenth century. Although their main goal—to permanently recapture the Holy Land—was never realized, the religious expeditions had several far-reaching effects on western Europe. First was the demand for such Eastern products as spices, sugar, and silk grew, which in turn led to a tremendous increase in trade. Second, the Greek church got so fed up at the crusaders that all hope of reuniting the eastern and western Christian churches was lost. And third, the Crusades introduced new methods and ideas, including an entire body of literature about the Crusades and their heroes, that contributed to massive changes brewing in western Europe.

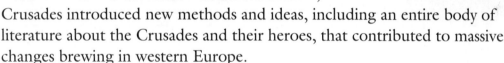

Name _____ Date _____

Interview a Crusader Knight

As you previously learned, newspapers did not exist in the Middle Ages. But if they had, don't you think it would have been interesting to interview a knight who had just returned from a Crusade?

Suppose you are a young reporter assigned to interview Sir Gallant, who has returned to France after several years in the Holy Land. What questions would you ask the local hero? How do you think he would respond to your questions?

After reading more about the Crusades in an encyclopedia or other source, write a short article reflecting your interview with the dashing Gallant. On the first line, give your story a title.

Title of your story

From *Everyday Life: The Middle Ages* © 2006 Good Year Books.

Name _____   Date _____

Solve a Puzzle about the Crusades

Fill in the sentences for clues to complete the puzzle about the Crusades.

```
_ _ C _ _ _ _ _
_ R _ _ _ _
_ U _ _ _
_ _ _ S _ _ _
_ A _ _ _ _
_ _ D _
_ E _ _ _
S _ _ _ _ _ _
```

1. King _____ of England was known as "The Lion-Hearted."

2. _____ II was pope when the Crusades began.

3. The _____ conquered the Holy Land in the eleventh century.

4. The Holy Land was in the region known as _____.

5. _____ the Penniless was a poor knight who helped lead a Crusade.

6. The Crusades led to an increase in _____ between Europe and the Middle East.

7. Peter the _____ helped lead the first unofficial crusade to the Holy Land.

8. _____ was a shepherd boy who led a group of French youngsters into thinking they could recapture the Holy Land from the Turks.

Name _____ Date _____

Make Complete Sentences of Fragments

All of the statements on this page are fragments. They are not sentences because they lack a subject, a verb, or some other necessary part. Rewrite each as a complete sentence on the line provided.

1. When people went on Crusades.

   _____

2. As Peter the Hermit began to speak.

   _____

3. Before the Holy Land had fallen to the Turks.

   _____

4. A poor knight such as Walter.

   _____

5. The Peasants' Crusade, a disastrous failure.

   _____

6. Frederick Barbarossa, Holy Roman Emperor.

   _____

7. Richard and Philip Augustus arguing over leadership.

   _____

8. Children setting out for the Holy Land.

   _____

9. As Stephen and his followers approached the Mediterranean Sea.

   _____

10. No sooner had Pope Urban II preached a Crusade.

    _____

11. The failure to recapture the Holy Land.

    _____

From *Everyday Life: The Middle Ages* © 2006 Good Year Books.

Name _____ Date _____

Look Up Facts about Islam

While Europe foundered in the Dark Ages during the early part of the medieval period, a great civilization existed in what is today called the Middle East. The Middle East is where the continents of Africa, Asia, and Europe meet. The civilization of which we speak was that of the Moslem, or Muslim, world.

How much do you know about the Muslims or of Islam, their religion? Consult an encyclopedia or some other source and answer the questions below.

1. Who is Muhammad?
_____

2. What is another name for Islam?
_____

3. What do the Muslims call God?
_____

4. What is the chief holy city of the Muslims?
_____

5. What do the Muslims believe about Jesus?
_____

6. What is a Muslim expected to do five times a day?
_____

7. What is the Koran (or Qur'an)?
_____

8. What is a mosque?
_____

9. What are all Muslims expected to do once in their lifetime (if they can)?
_____

10. Rounded to the nearest million, there were some 3,000,000 people of Muslim faith living in the United States in 2005. Out of a total population of about 296,000,000, what percentage are Muslim? Write your answer on the line at the bottom.

_____ percent

CHAPTER 9

Medieval Towns

P icture yourself and a friend walking happily down a street in a town of medieval times. Together you are discussing plans for the evening, and neither of you has any idea of the catastrophe that is about to unfold.

As you round a corner, you hear a shrill voice coming from the window of a house six stories above the street. The voice belongs to a lady issuing a warning that roughly translates into "look out below!" Before you can take evasive action, you are suddenly drenched with a bucket of gooey garbage. Your nose tells you it is a mixture of black pudding, beans, and the remains of eels the family on the sixth floor had for dinner.

A priest prays for victims of the plague. Those who became ill often died within hours.

Do you angrily make your way up to the room from whence came the garbage and express your displeasure? Do you threaten to punch the lady's husband in the nose? Of course not. You brush yourself off as best you can and go on your way. If anyone is to be scolded, it is you for not having jumped out of the way quickly enough.

Garbage (and worse) being thrown into the street was a common practice in medieval towns. Even birth and rank held no privilege when it came to being hit with something unpleasant. No less a person than King Louis IX of France was himself doused with the contents of a chamber pot while strolling along a Paris street one fine day.

In the absence of any kind of sanitation service, people did the natural thing and tossed their waste wherever it might fall. Had they realized the health threats involved they surely would have acted differently. As it was, they relied on pigs and other animals that roamed free to take the place of the present-day garbage truck. Sometimes a particularly hard rain would help by washing away some of the refuse.

It is only natural that under such unsanitary conditions disease would run rampant. Epidemics that took the lives of large portions of the populations of medieval villages and towns were common. One such epidemic of the bubonic

From *Everyday Life: The Middle Ages* © 2006 Good Year Books.

plague in the fourteenth century wiped out not only entire towns but possibly a third of the population of Europe. That was the dreaded "Black Death" that appeared in Europe in the year 1347.

Bubonic plague is a disease transmitted to humans by fleas from rats. When the disease appears today anywhere in the world, it can quickly be brought under control. During the Middle Ages, however, neither the nature of the disease nor a treatment for it were known. When it struck, its victims died almost immediately. Many people went to bed perfectly healthy and died before the sun rose the next day. The term *Black Death* came from the fact that black spots appeared on the bodies of all who contracted it. Before it ran its course, the disease took the lives of some fifty million people.

The series of plagues that swept Europe actually played a role in weakening feudalism. The dramatic population decline led to a severe labor shortage, making serfs' and peasants' labor much more valuable. Therefore, they were able to negotiate more rights and better conditions from their lords. In addition, the population of towns recovered more rapidly, so towns became more important than feudal estates.

Although towns in the Middle Ages were dirty, unsafe, and dangerous, they represented a step forward from the instability of the Dark Ages. The uncertainty of feudal life caused people to seek safety either near the castle of a powerful lord or on the grounds of some remote monastery. This need for safety actually led to the reappearance of towns. As more and more people gathered around places that could afford them protection, castle and monastery grounds began to take on the appearance of villages. In time these villages became towns. As these towns grew in population and prospered, many were able to buy their freedom from the feudal lord who controlled them. Others won their independence through armed uprisings. A dramatic increase in population in the twelfth century also led to more urbanizations.

More towns appeared as travel became safer and trade increased. Some towns sprang up at crossroads, where traders and merchants came and went. Others developed near rivers or along seacoasts. Some towns, such as Paris, France, and Florence, Italy, were quite large. Most, however, averaged between five thousand and ten thousand people in population.

Towns that developed while national governments were weak and conditions were still unstable had high walls for protection. It was the presence of such walls that made medieval towns crowded. With only so much ground space available, it was necessary to construct buildings as high as six and seven

stories. As each story was added, the builder extended it out somewhat over the street to make it larger. By the time the building reached the sixth or seventh level, the occupant of the top floor could literally reach out and touch the building across the street. How's that for close neighbors?

It was this closeness of the buildings that made fire an ever-present threat. Because most structures until the Renaissance period were built of wood, fire spread quickly once it started. Some towns were partially or totally destroyed by fire a number of times. London burned four times in the twelfth century, and Rouen, France, the city where Joan of Arc was burned at the stake in 1431, was totally consumed six times between 1200 and 1225. Later, when stone was used for construction and fire brigades introduced, the number of fires were reduced dramatically.

Monteriggioni, in Tuscany, Italy, is an example of a walled town from the later Middle Ages.

Appearance-wise, medieval towns were generally laid out in the same way. In the center was a large open area variously referred to as a square, a place, or a piazza. If the town was very large, the square might also be the location of a cathedral. Towns squares were hubs of activity where tradesmen and merchants set up stalls and conducted business. Sometimes strolling actors drew crowds as they performed a play for all who would stop and listen. So too did jugglers, tumblers, and clowns. Between 8:00 and 9:00 P.M. the curfew bell rang, and most citizens retired for the night behind the safety of their doors. Streets were dark and danger ever-present, and there were few policemen to guarantee the safety of any person who dared to venture out. Those who did were required to carry a light and have a good reason to be outside.

Who were the inhabitants of these early towns? Most were members of a new middle class of merchants, traders, and craftsmen referred to as the *bourgeoisie. Bourgeoisie* is a French term meaning "town dweller." In the German language, the term becomes *burgher* or *burger.* A free town with the right of self-government was called a *borough,* or in German *burg.* You are probably beginning to see the influence on America by now. What about

From *Everyday Life: The Middle Ages* © 2006 Good Year Books.

Pittsburgh and *Harrisburg*? And *hamburger*? Supposedly, immigrants from the German city of Hamburg brought that American favorite with them when they arrived in the 1800s.

The merchants and craftsmen monopolized business within the walls of a city. They formed guilds, which in some ways resembled early labor unions. Membership in the appropriate guild was mandatory for all merchants and craftsmen. A young man had to pass through a training stage before becoming a full-fledged member. First, beginning about the age of seven, a boy desiring to learn a trade was apprenticed to a master craftsman. When he acquired the skills to earn a living, he became a journeyman. As such, he could then work for anyone who would hire him. If he wanted to become a master craftsman and own his own shop, he had to pass a strict exam supervised by leading members of the guild. This involved creating a masterpiece of work showing that he had mastered his particular skill.

A guild master judging the skills of two journeymen.

Merchant and craft guilds became increasingly powerful through the Middle Ages as towns grew. Whereas knights lived for war, peace and stability were in the best interests of traders and craftsmen who wanted to conduct a profitable business. Therefore, town guilds often supported the king against troublemaking nobles, further weakening the feudal system.

Most of the other inhabitants of medieval cities were laborers who took any job they could find. These included serfs who had either run away from the manor or had been granted their freedom. Each town also had its share of beggars and thieves, both of whom preyed on the local citizenry. With streets so crowded and so many people about, a fast thief with an even faster knife could cut a purse away from a belt in record time and be gone in a flash. Towns did their best to discourage such lawbreakers, even leaving executed criminals hanging from the gallows indefinitely. Paris, for example, always had twenty-four bodies swinging at the end of ropes for all to see. The message to passersby was simple: Behave yourself while in our town or face the consequences!

Such was life in typical towns of the Middle Ages.

Name _____ Date _____

Research Bubonic Plague

Some information about bubonic plague was presented in chapter 9. Find out more about this terrible disease by consulting an encyclopedia or some other source. Then answer these six questions.

1. What causes bubonic plague?

   _____

   _____

2. How is the plague transmitted?

   _____

   _____

3. List any four symptoms of the plague.

   _____ _____

   _____ _____

4. How is the plague treated in modern times?

   _____

   _____

5. How can the plague be prevented or at least kept from spreading?

   _____

   _____

6. To refer to the Black Death of the Middle Ages solely as an epidemic is not entirely correct. Epidemics may be either *endemic* or *pandemic*. Look up each word in a dictionary and write its meaning. Then tell whether the Black Death of the Middle Ages was endemic or pandemic in nature.

   _____

   _____

   _____

   _____

   _____

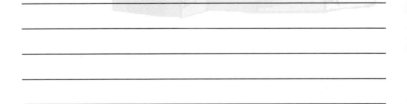

Name _____ Date _____

Finish a Story

When the Black Death struck a community or town in the 1300s, people panicked. They did not know what caused the disease and they had no idea how to treat it. Many thought it was God's punishment for their sins. Whatever they believed, they often fled to the countryside, hoping to avoid exposure to what was almost certain death.

Imagine you are living in an English town during the bubonic plague epidemic of the 1340s. One day, while watching the ships come in at the docks, you see a vessel run aground a short distance away. A quick check by dock workers reveals the terrible truth: The entire crew has succumbed to the Black Death.

Complete the story that has been started for you. Give it any kind of ending you prefer. Continue on a separate sheet of paper if necessary.

Thomas and I watched the grounded ship with a mixture of curiosity and horror. Even at our young age, we suspected what a group of men who boarded the ship soon confirmed.

"The Black Death! The Black Death!" they shouted as they fled in the direction of the town. "The Black Death!"

Upon seeing the panic and terror in their faces, Thomas and I too turned and ran as fast as our legs could carry us. Mother saw us approaching from a window and greeted us at the door.

"Thomas! Jonathan! What in the world is the matter?"

"It's the plague, Mother! The plague is here!"

_____
_____
_____
_____
_____
_____
_____
_____
_____
_____
_____
_____
_____
_____
_____

From *Everyday Life: The Middle Ages* © 2006 Good Year Books.

Name _____ Date _____

Fill in a Venn Diagram

Fill in the Venn diagram to compare towns in the Middle Ages with cities today. Write facts about each in the appropriate place. Where the circles overlap, list features common to both.

Towns in the Middle Ages

Both

Cities Today

From *Everyday Life: The Middle Ages* © 2006 Good Year Books.

Name _____ Date _____

Interpret a Bar Graph

The following graph shows the estimated populations of five European cities around the year 1300. The cities are Paris, France; Florence, Italy; Modena, Italy; York, England; Nuremberg, Germany; and Cologne, Germany.

Use the information from the graph and answer the questions at the bottom of the page. It might be helpful to review the terms *mode, range,* and *median* in your mathematics book before proceeding.

Write your answers on the lines following the questions.

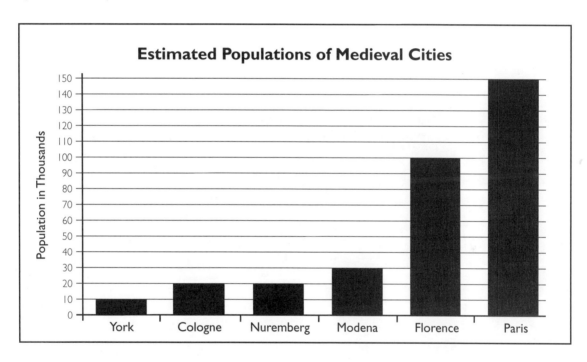

Estimated Populations of Medieval Cities

1. How many times greater was the population of Paris than that of York?
   _____ times greater.
2. What mode is represented by the population figures on the graph? _____
3. What is the range? _____
4. What is the average population of the six cities? _____
5. Why can you state that no median is represented by the numbers on the graph?

_____

CHAPTER 10

Schools and Universities

Dear Dad,

Well, I'm broke again! You know how it is here on campus; everything is so expensive. Then when you add in trips to the supermarket, the laundromat, the barber shop, and other places, the money just gives out.

So, Dad, if you can spare it, could you deposit another hundred dollars in my account until next Friday? I'd really appreciate it.

Love,

Tommy

Sound familiar? The above brief letter might have been written by any student at any college or university in the United States. But it wasn't; it was written by a French student to his father sometime during the thirteenth century. (The original was written in verse, but it is rewritten here so you can better understand it.)

Students in the universities of medieval Europe seemed always in need of money, much like their modern-day counterparts. Some even resorted to begging to eat and pay for their studies. But more about this later. First, we will take a quick look at the schools students attended before they entered a university.

Few schools existed in the early Middle Ages. Those that did were run by monasteries or churches. They taught students hymns in Latin, basic reading and writing, music, and etiquette and courtesy, generally in preparation to become either monks or clergymen. As a rule, only boys of noble families attended, although occasionally the bright son of a peasant might be admitted, if his lord permitted. A few well-to-do girls received a basic education from nuns at convent schools. Some well-to-do fathers also hired tutors to educate their boys and sometimes girls at home. Most teachers had reputations for being extremely harsh and beating students who didn't learn their lessons.

Boys and girls who had no desire to enter the religious life often received little or no education. Many noble boys trained to become knights, a profession in which an education was not deemed necessary. Some noble lads learned to read, but few of them mastered the art of writing beyond their names. Daughters of noble parents were taught what they needed to know to manage a household. As for other children, some young boys were apprenticed to master craftsmen to learn a trade. All that the children of serfs needed to

From *Everyday Life: The Middle Ages* © 2006 Good Year Books.

know was how to perform the various tasks required of them on the manor and to give the correct responses during the Latin church service.

As towns grew, universities began to appear on the scene. They had their beginnings in a most unusual way: any scholar who believed he had worthwhile knowledge to impart and who could attract a following of students could set himself up as a school. Students paid him a fee and usually met at his house or at a rented room for instruction. Often renowned teachers clustered in cathedral towns, forming communities of scholars.

By the twelfth century, there were enough students and teachers to form universities. The University of Bologna was the first European university, founded in 1088. The second was the University of Paris in 1150. Early universities specialized in one or two fields. Bologna was a school of law, while the University of Salerno in southern Italy was a medical school. The University of Paris in France emphasized philosophy and theology, as did Oxford and Cambridge in England. Boys entered the university around fourteen years of age and studied core liberal arts for six years: verbal arts (called the *trivium*) and the quadrivium of arithmetic, astronomy, geometry, and music. If they passed an oral examination by the master under whom they had studied, they could pursue master's or doctoral degrees in the university's specialized subjects, such as law.

This doorway, from a building at the University of Bologna, shows the faces of the Former Rectors of the University. The school is thought to be the oldest university in Europe.

You will be interested to learn that some universities were started and run by the students themselves on the model of a guild. The University of Bologna in Italy was founded in this way. Students hired and paid the teachers. They also fined or fired those who did not live up to their standards or who displeased them in any way. For example, any professor who failed to show up for class or who left important material out of a lecture could expect to pay a fine. Even in the early days before universities became formally organized, students would often attend several lectures and "size up" a teacher before paying him his fee.

From Everyday Life: The Middle Ages © 2006 Good Year Books.

Medieval universities differed from those today in several ways. When students gathered at the teacher's house for instruction, they found no chairs or desks, so they sat on the floor. Often the floor was covered with straw to guard against the dampness. Still, trying to learn in an unheated room in winter was a difficult task. Sometimes students' hands became so numb from the cold that they could not write. In such cases, they simply listened to the teacher lecture or read from a book.

All teaching in medieval schools was by lecture. Here, medieval students are shown paying close attention to their instructor.

Actually, it might be more accurate to say that the teacher read from *the* book rather than *a* book. Usually there was only one book in a classroom. More than likely it was a rare manuscript hand-copied by a monk in a monastery. With books so scarce, only the teacher was in possession of one. Students listened intently and copied down everything their instructor read or said. If they paid strict attention and concentrated on their copying, they would, at the end of a particular course, be in possession of their very own book. (Even when universities began to meet in regular classrooms, their libraries often contained only a few books. And these were always chained to a desk or shelf to prevent their being stolen.)

In addition to not having regular classrooms, early universities also contained no dormitories or other places of residence. Students found lodging as best they could, often renting rooms from unscrupulous landlords at prices they could ill-afford. Beginning in the twelfth century, students began living together in "colleges" to get a break on rent and food. Not only was rent in university towns high, food was so expensive and other conditions so unsatisfactory that violence by students was common. Both Paris and Oxford recorded many accounts of riots between students and townspeople. Sometimes tension reached the point that a group of teachers and students would leave one university and found another. The University of Oxford was founded in this manner following a particularly severe riot in Paris. And

Cambridge was founded when some teachers and students at Oxford grew weary of continual conflict between students and townspeople there.

In time, residence halls were provided for students, and their daily routines were more closely supervised. They rose at 4:00 or 5:00 in the morning and attended Mass from 5:00 to 6:00. After Mass, they attended classes until 10:00. At 10:00 they ate their first meal of the day, which might consist of soup and a small amount of beef. Then followed more classes until about 5:00 in the afternoon, at which time they ate a supper no more filling than their first meal. The period between supper and about 10:00 at night was devoted to study. At 10:00, students retired, but not before undergoing certain preparations. One Cambridge student reported that he walked or ran about for some time to avoid going to bed with cold feet.

Students who lived in dormitories were expected to adhere to other rules as well. They were forbidden to gamble or to use profanity, and they would be fined if they broke curfew. As is true at modern universities, some students chose to ignore as many rules as they could. They caroused through the town late at night, violated curfew hours, and made nuisances of themselves everywhere they went. In the Church-run universities, students were under the protection of the clergy and could literally get away with murder in the town.

Some students were the sons of nobles and merchants who had sufficient money and who had no problem making ends meet. Others came from poor families who could offer them little help. These students took any job they could find to help pay their expenses. Those who could not find work often resorted, as mentioned earlier, to begging or singing in the streets for a handout. Many even looked forward to summer vacations when they could devote full time to being vagabond beggars.

Marble sculpture of students at the University of Bologna. Because students there hired their teachers, they could also decide to dock a teacher's pay.

Name _____ Date _____

Create University-related Word Problems

Medieval historians varied greatly in their estimates of the number of students that attended early universities. One guessed that in 1300 the enrollment of the University of Paris was 7,000, that of Bologna 6,000, and that of Oxford 3,000. Another elevated these figures substantially. He placed the number of students at both Paris and Oxford at 30,000 and those at Bologna 10,000. In the spaces provided, use these figures to create two word problems. Ask a classmate to solve them.

Problem #1

_____

_____

_____

Answer _____

Problem #2

_____

_____

_____

Answer _____

In 2004, the average cost for a student to attend one year of college in the United States was about $11,354. In 1347, an Oxford student reported spending, in present U.S. dollars, a total of $1,280 for a year of instruction. Again, use the information given to create two word problems in the spaces provided and ask a classmate to solve them.

Problem #1

_____

_____

_____

Answer _____

Problem #2

_____

_____

_____

Answer _____

From Everyday Life: The Middle Ages © 2006 GoodYear Books.

Name _____ Date _____

Write Your Thoughts to These Questions

Think about the questions presented here. Then write your best answer to each.

1. Historians have said that students in the Middle Ages might have been less rowdy and more cooperative had early universities featured athletic teams and extracurricular activities as colleges do today. Do you agree or disagree with this belief? Why or why not? How might sporting events and other activities lessen incidents of misbehavior?

    _____

    _____

    _____

2. Why do you think theology (the study of religion) was the principal course of study at many medieval universities?

    _____

    _____

    _____

3. Students in the Middle Ages were limited in their choices of universities to attend. By contrast, students today have hundreds of colleges and universities competing for their enrollment. Some of these schools are small; others are quite large. Each size has advantages that the other cannot match. Think of three advantages of each and write them on the lines provided.

    Small colleges

    _____

    _____

    _____

    Large universities

    _____

    _____

    _____

Name _____ Date _____

Distinguish between Fact and Opinion

Can you tell a fact from an opinion? A fact is something known to be true. An opinion is simply what someone thinks.

On the blank line before each of these statements, write F if you consider it a fact or O if you think it is an opinion.

1. _____ Students in the Middle Ages took education more seriously than students do today.

2. _____ Instructors in medieval universities were better qualified to teach than are their modern counterparts.

3. _____ Uncomfortable classrooms sometimes made learning in a medieval university difficult.

4. _____ The University of Bologna specialized in the study of law.

5. _____ Instruction in today's colleges and universities would be much better if students hired and fired teachers.

6. _____ The lecture method of instruction is far superior to all other methods.

7. _____ The University of Salerno was primarily a school of medicine.

8. _____ Books were scarce in the Middle Ages.

9. _____ Today's college students manage their finances better than students in the Middle Ages.

10. _____ Everyone today should be given the opportunity to attend college.

11. _____ Students who lived in the residence halls of medieval universities were placed under strict supervision.

12. _____ Some medieval college students resorted to begging to defray the cost of their education.

13. _____ All students today should receive financial help from the government to attend college.

From *Everyday Life: The Middle Ages* © 2006 Good Year Books.

Name _____ Date _____

Complete a Word Search

In the word box below are nineteen words from chapter 10. Find and circle each in the word search. They run horizontally, vertically, and diagonally. None are inverted, or backward. In your search, you will find other words that are not from the chapter. Do not circle these words.

```
U X D C P E O P L E S A L E R N O
K N G O Q C E Y T Y V P A R I S X
T H I N R A D D M A R Y T L O W W
M O O V G M A N U S C R I P T H J
O K M E E B I A X C N N N B E A R
X S Q N P R K T H R A L M A R L X
F X T T R I S N O B B T C K L E M
O X T U L D S I Z R P Z I N A C F
R X Z K D G M S T V Y C B O T T F
D E G R E E K O X Y B C D W N U G
P E R S O N N G N S C H O L A R E
V V K N I G H T R K J A Y E L E X
M A R Y L A N D T E X A S D G O V
P E N S A C O L A B O L O G N A K
P E N N S Y L V A N I A X E G G G
```

BOLOGNA
CAMBRIDGE
CONVENT
DEGREE
DORMITORY
EDUCATION
KNIGHT
KNOWLEDGE
LATIN
LECTURE
MANUSCRIPT
MONK
OXFORD
PARIS
RIOT
SALERNO
SCHOLAR
STUDENT
UNIVERSITY

Failures and Achievements

The Medieval period saw major achievements in language, literature, philosophy, art, and architecture. But because of age-old superstitions and limited knowledge about the universe, less progress was made in science. Two "sciences" dominated medieval people's thinking. One was alchemy; the other was astrology. Alchemy was an attempt by scientific dabblers to turn various metals into gold. Astrology is the study of using the stars and planets to predict events. Neither is a true science, although in time the sciences of chemistry and astronomy grew out of them.

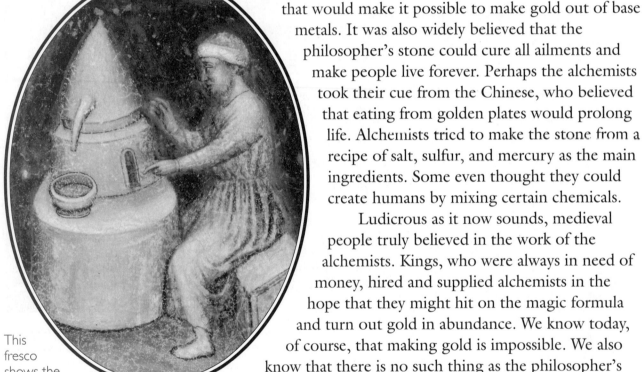

This fresco shows the alchemist at work trying to change other metals into gold. Alchemists also attempted to create humans from chemicals.

Medieval alchemists spent considerable time searching for the philosopher's stone. This was thought to be a substance that would make it possible to make gold out of base metals. It was also widely believed that the philosopher's stone could cure all ailments and make people live forever. Perhaps the alchemists took their cue from the Chinese, who believed that eating from golden plates would prolong life. Alchemists tried to make the stone from a recipe of salt, sulfur, and mercury as the main ingredients. Some even thought they could create humans by mixing certain chemicals.

Ludicrous as it now sounds, medieval people truly believed in the work of the alchemists. Kings, who were always in need of money, hired and supplied alchemists in the hope that they might hit on the magic formula and turn out gold in abundance. We know today, of course, that making gold is impossible. We also know that there is no such thing as the philosopher's stone and that it is impossible to create humans from chemicals or in some way make them live forever. But in the Middle Ages, most people believed all these things were possible.

Alchemy was closely linked to astrology. Both alchemists and astrologers believed that each metal was controlled by a particular planet. The sun, for example, was thought to represent gold. Silver was controlled by the moon, and the other planets were linked to various metals in kind. Alchemists also believed that the positions of the planets would determine their success and failure in discovering the elusive philosopher's stone.

Astrology is a study that is even older than alchemy. The rulers of ancient Egypt and other early civilizations had official astrologers who advised them on their every move. Dates for battles and other important events were determined by what astrologers reported. In the same way, the people of the Middle Ages believed that the positions of the stars and planets influenced their daily lives. (Even in modern times, leaders have consulted astrologers before taking decisive steps.)

Although alchemists and astrologers failed in what they were trying to accomplish, their efforts were not in vain. As previously mentioned, their work led to the development of the sciences of chemistry and astronomy. Alchemists not only accidentally discovered many kinds of chemicals but they also stumbled upon medicines that proved effective in treating certain illnesses. Astrologers, for their part, made discoveries that led later scientists to study the heavens for reasons other than trying to predict the future. Out of such studies emerged astronomy and a wealth of knowledge about the universe in which we live.

Dante Alighieri, also known simply as Dante, author of *The Divine Comedy*.

Lack of progress in science could not be blamed on Roger Bacon. Bacon was an English monk who was far ahead of his time in thinking and theory. Many people considered him some kind of wizard because of his predictions about the future. Before he died in 1292, Bacon had envisioned such modern innovations as horseless carriages and submarines. He also thought that people would someday be able to fly. Perhaps his greatest contribution was his advocating (recommending) observation and experimentation in solving scientific problems. This was a novel idea in the Middle Ages, when the Bible was used as the source of authority for tackling any issue.

While progress in science was hampered by superstition and religious boundaries, notable achievements were made in fields such as literature and language. You may have heard of the writers Dante and Chaucer. Dante is remembered for his *Divine Comedy*, which deals with an imaginary trip through

From *Everyday Life: The Middle Ages* © 2006 Good Year Books.

Hell, Purgatory, and Heaven. Chaucer is most famous for his *Canterbury Tales*, a collection of short stories told by a group of pilgrims on their way to a shrine in Canterbury, England.

What Dante and Chaucer wrote is not as important as how they wrote it. Both used the vernacular, or the everyday, spoken language of their people. In doing so, they helped set standards of spelling and structure that became the foundations of modern Italian and English. Writers in France, Germany, and other countries also began writing in their native languages.

About the year 1450, almost at the end of the Middle Ages, a German named Johannes Gutenberg invented the printing press. Printing was not new, for printing with wooden blocks had been developed by the Chinese centuries earlier. What made Gutenberg's press unique and revolutionary was that it used movable type. Letters could be set in any order and used over again, making it possible to print numerous copies of books cheaply. Printing presses used Gutenberg's basic design into the twentieth century.

Writing in a native language made it easier for more people to learn to read. (The invention of eyeglasses also helped!) The printing press, in turn, made more books available. These together brought about a decline in illiteracy. Coupled with the rise of universities, they were significant factors in bringing on that revival of interest in learning known as the Renaissance.

No achievement of medieval people has proven more enduring than their beautiful Gothic cathedrals. You may remember from an activity at the end of chapter 6 that Renaissance architects labeled such cathedrals "Gothic" because they considered them barbaric in construction. But from the twelfth to the sixteenth centuries, their style dominated religious architecture everywhere. More than five hundred Gothic cathedrals and churches were built in France alone.

The construction of large Gothic cathedrals sometimes took more than one hundred years. Some were never finished. Money and labor to build these "Monuments to God" came from every class. Wealthy nobles donated huge sums toward their completion. Peasants from the countryside provided the back-breaking free labor to haul large stones from quarries to building sites. And a variety of artisans possessed the skills and the craftsmanship that made the buildings possible. These included stonecutters, carpenters, sculptors, masons, and workers in metal and stained glass. All who labored on a cathedral were under the supervision of an architect, who, for his services, usually received free housing, an exemption from taxes, and a large bonus when the project was completed.

From *Everyday Life: The Middle Ages* © 2006 Good Year Books.

Gothic cathedrals were medieval people's answer to the rather plain-looking Romanesque (named after the Romans) cathedrals of the early Middle Ages. Romanesque architecture emphasized thick walls, domed ceilings, round arches, and few windows. In contrast, the Gothic style stressed relatively thin walls, high ceilings, pointed arches, and an abundance of stained-glass windows. The thin walls and high ceilings were supported on the outside by braces called *flying buttresses.*

The use of flying buttresses allowed architects to reduce the size of wall needed to support the building, making room for the stained-glass windows that make Gothic cathedrals so beautiful and unique. The cathedral at Chartres, France, contains 176 individual windows, each telling in colored pictures a story from the Bible. Craftsmen made the brilliant colors used in the windows from various metallic oxides.

By the end of the sixteenth century, when Gothic architecture ceased, Europe was on the brink of modern times. Feudalism was long dead and kings had reestablished their authority throughout the continent. Explorers were sailing the oceans, bringing back news of distant lands and proving that the world was indeed round. An exciting period called the Renaissance had begun, introducing new ideas and ways of life that changed Europe forever. In a word, the Middle Ages were over.

The beautiful Gothic cathedral at Chartres, France, contains 176 windows, each of which shows a story from the Bible.

Name _____ Date _____

Use Context Clues to Complete Sentences

Fill in the sentences on the page with words from the word box.

| advice |
| bad |
| cause |
| common |
| contributions |
| cured |
| every |
| except |
| health |
| however |
| magic |
| modern |
| often |
| precious |
| procedure |
| vein |

You learned in chapter 11 that the people of the Middle Ages made few _____ in science. The same held true in related fields such as medicine.

Medieval medicine consisted of a combination of religious faith and superstition. Demons were believed to _____ disease, and an ailment could be _____ only through prayer and ritual. The wearing of amulets, or _____ charms, to ward off evil and demons was a _____ practice of the times. So too was bloodletting, a favorite _____ of medieval physicians. In bloodletting, a specific _____ was opened to treat a particular illness. Unfortunately, this completely useless technique continued well into _____ times.

For good _____ and well-being, medieval doctors offered _____ that is amusing to us today. They instructed patients, for example, not to drink milk or eat cheese and nuts _____ on rare occasions. They also insisted that raw onions eaten in the evening would have a _____ effect on the mind and the senses.

From a hygiene standpoint, the good doctors advised people against bathing too _____. Frequent baths, they maintained, washed away _____ body oils that protected one from illness. Washing the hair _____ two weeks, _____, was good practice, providing it was done with hot lye.

I think you would agree that medical science has come a long way since the Middle Ages.

From *Everyday Life: The Middle Ages* © 2006 Good Year Books.

Name _____ Date _____

Draw a Gothic Cathedral

In the space provided on the page, make a rough drawing of a Gothic cathedral. Consult your textbook, an encyclopedia, or some other source for examples.

On the lines at the bottom, list any three prominent features of the Gothic style of architecture.

Characteristics of the Gothic style

1. _____
2. _____
3. _____

Name _____ Date _____

Write an Essay

Write an essay beginning with these words in bold type: **"If the printing press with movable type had never been invented...."**

Try to imagine where humankind might be today with regard to progress (or the lack of it) without this invention.

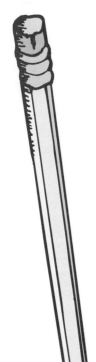

From Everyday Life: The Middle Ages © 2006 Good Year Books.

Name _____   Date _____

Make an Outline

The following partially completed outline highlights in bold letters some important topics covered in your study of the Middle Ages. Beside the numbers listed under each, write two subtopics you think would go along with the topic. The first one is done for you.

A. Feudalism

1. Breakdown of law and order
2. Life centered around castles and manor houses

B. Life on a Manor

1. _____
2. _____

C. Knights and Knighthood

1. _____
2. _____

D. The Medieval Church

1. _____
2. _____

E. Fun and Amusements

1. _____
2. _____

F. The Crusades

1. _____
2. _____

G. Medieval Towns

1. _____
2. _____

H. Schools and Universities

1. _____
2. _____

I. Cultural Achievements

1. _____
2. _____

Answers to Activities

Chapter 1

Recall Information You Have Read

1. feudalism: political, economic, and social system that characterized Europe during most of the Middle Ages
2. vassal: a noble who received land from a higher lord
3. overlord: a lord who granted land to another lord in return for certain services
4. fief: a piece of land granted by one lord to another
5. homage: the formal acknowledgement of loyalty from a vassal to his lord
6. Vikings: raiders from Scandinavia who terrorized Europe in the ninth and tenth centuries
7. serf: a peasant bound to a piece of land
8. aqueduct: a device for carrying water a great distance
9. Visigoths: German tribe that conquered Rome
10. Charlemagne: Frankish king who restored order in western Europe in the late eighth and early ninth centuries

Solve a Feudalism Puzzle

1. fief 2. serf 3. aqueduct 4. overlord 5. vassal
6. Charlemagne 7. Vikings 8. Visigoths 9. homage

Do a Scan of Scandinavia

1. The name possibly came from *Scandia,* the name the ancient Romans gave to the region. Other researchers think the origin may be from *Skane,* a province of southern Sweden. 2. Norway: Oslo; Denmark: Copenhagen; Iceland: Reykjavik; Sweden: Stockholm; Finland: Helsinki 3. Sweden and Finland 4. Baltic 5. Denmark 6. Russia 7. Germany 8. Atlantic 9. Finns; Norwegians; Danes; Icelanders; Swedes

Chapter 2

Make Inferences from Facts

Students' answers should be similar to the following:
1. Not all serfs were farmers.
2. Serfs knew little of the world beyond the manor.
3. The lord did no work himself.
4. The ring allowed a runaway serf to be returned to the proper master.
5. Some serfs plowed their fields using nothing more than muscle power.

Fill in a Venn Diagram

Students' answers should be similar to the following:
Medieval Serfs: were bound to the soil; could not be sold separately; rented strips of land themselves
Both: had few rights; labored long hours; were severely punished if they tried to run away
Plantation Slaves: could be sold as individuals; owned no land or property themselves

Chapter 3

Solve a Castle Puzzle

Across: 1. mutton 3. drawbridge 7. catapult 8. keep 11. feasts 12. minstrel 13. chess
Down: 1. moat 2. jester 4. bailey 5. ram 6. Hall 9. portcullis 10. venison

Help Lord Snootville Eat Better

Students' answers should be similar to the following:
1. high blood pressure
2. It can cause strokes and other health problems.
3. Hypertension is treated through drugs, exercise, and diet.
4. a fatty substance found throughout the blood and tissues of the body
5. Some cholesterol is referred to as "bad cholesterol" and can result in hardening of the arteries, leading to a heart attack.
6. By exercise and by limiting foods high in cholesterol. In addition, medication is often necessary.

Chapter 4

Make False Statements True

1. quintain 2. page 3. twenty-one 4. hauberk
5. flail 6. red 7. cap or hat 8. gold 9. ladies
10. care for his lord's horses and armor 11. squires
12. sword 13. some; a few 14. horseman or knight

Chapter 5

Use Context Clues to Complete Sentences

important; invented; glorify; understand; exception; continued; shores; elsewhere; Earth; added; based; tales; latter; backward; collection; beliefs

Name Those Synonyms and Antonyms

Students' answers will vary, but examples are listed.

From *Everyday Life: The Middle Ages* © 2006 Good Year Books.

1. desired; renounced 2. far; near 3. praising; criticizing 4. praise; condemn 5. enjoyed; disliked 6. faithful; disloyal 7. well liked; unpopular 8. look up to; detest 9. call; dismiss 10. brave; cowardly 11. much; little 12. sound; illogical 13. frequently; seldom 14. nearly; absolutely 15. draw; repel 16. exceptional; commonplace 17. unpleasant; pleasant 18. magnified; understated 19. embrace; omit 20. genuine; false

Chapter 6

Draw Conclusions from What You Have Read

Answers will vary but should be similar to the following:

1. He was possibly trying to prove that he was pure and free of sin.
2. The achievements of the Greek and Roman worlds might have been lost forever.
3. She does not want her husband to break the Church's Truce of God, which forbade fighting between Wednesday evening and Monday morning.

Solve Some Cathedral Math

1. 123.5   2. 21   3. 35; 37; 38; 42

Recall Information You Have Read

1. early period of the Middle Ages following the fall of the Roman Empire
2. word meaning "universal"
3. eastern part of the Christian Church after it split in 1054
4. sacred religious ceremonies of the Christian Church
5. the act of cutting off a person from the services of the Church
6. cutting off an entire region or country from the services of the Church
7. Church decree that prohibited fighting around designated places
8. Church decree that forbade fighting between Wednesday evening and Monday morning and on religious holidays
9. person who shuns society and lives alone in some remote area
10. beautifully decorated, hand-copied book

Chapter 7

Compare Then and Now

Students' answers will vary but should be similar to the following:

Medieval Tournaments/Modern Sporting Events
   Similarities: people sat in stands; musicians played; much excitement and cheering
   Differences: winners kept personal belongings of losers; contestants were sometimes purposely killed; nobility and commoners sat separately

Medieval Fairs/Modern Fairs
   Similarities: exhibits of goods; entertainment; laughter and gaiety
   Differences: traveling merchants sold goods from stalls; were at first held outside castles and monasteries; might last as long as six weeks

Complete a Vocabulary Exercise

1. a 2. b 3. a 4. b 5. c 6. a 7. c 8. a 9. c 10. b

Chapter 8

Solve a Puzzle about the Crusades

1. Richard 2. Urban 3. Turks 4. Palestine 5. Walter 6. trade 7. Hermit 8. Stephen

Make Complete Sentences of Fragments

Students' answers will vary.

Look Up Facts about Islam

1. the founder of Islam and its chief prophet.
2. Muhammadanism 3. Allah 4. Mecca
5. that he was a prophet but not the son of God
6. pray 7. the Muslim holy book 8. a Muslim place of worship 9. go on a pilgrimage to Mecca
10. about 1%

Chapter 9

Research Bubonic Plague

Students' answers should be similar to the following:

1. a bacterium called *Yersinia pestis*
2. by fleas that bite infected rats
3. chills and fever; headache; body pains; swelling of lymph glands in neck, groin, and armpits
4. with such drugs as tetracycline and streptomycin
5. through sanitation and rat control, isolating patients, and taking antibiotics if you might have been exposed

Everyday Life: The Middle Ages

6. endemic—found in a particular locale; pandemic—affecting a large number of the population over a wide area. The Black Death was pandemic.

Fill in a Venn Diagram

Answers will vary but should be similar to the following:

Towns in the Middle Ages: dirty; unsafe; small and crowded; fire hazards; bustling; dark; buildings made of wood

Both: crowded (some); dirty and unsafe (some); bustling

Cities Today: street lights; cars, taxis, buses, etc.; police; larger in size; buildings of brick or stone or metal

Interpret a Bar Graph

1. 15 2. 20,000 3. 140,000 4. 55,000
5. No figure falls in the middle.

Chapter 10
Write Your Thoughts to the Questions Below

Students' answers will vary.

Distinguish between Fact and Opinion

1. O 2. O 3. F 4. F 5. O 6. O 7. F 8. F
9. O 10. O 11. F 12. F 13. O

Complete a Word Search

```
U X D C P E O P L E S A L E R N O
K N G O Q C E Y T Y V P A R I S X
T H I N R A D D M A R Y T L O W W
M O O V G M A N U S C R I P T H J
O K M E E B I A X C N N N B E A R
X S Q N P R K T H R A L M A R L X
F X T T R I S N O B B T C K L E M
O X T U L D S I Z R P Z I N A C F
R X Z K D G M S T V Y C B O T T F
D E G R E E K O X Y B C D W N U G
P E R S O N N G N S C H O L A R E
V V K N I G H T R K J A Y E L E X
M A R Y L A N D T E X A S D G O V
P E N S A C O L A B O L O G N A K
P E N N S Y L V A N I A X E G G G
```

Chapter 11
Use Context Clues to Complete Sentences

contributions; cause; cured; magic; common; procedure; vein; modern; health; advice; except; bad; often; precious; every; however

Additional Resources

Books for Children

Clifford, Alan. *The Middle Ages*. St. Paul, Minnesota: Greenhaven Press, Inc., 1980.
Dambrosio, Monica, and Roberto Barbieri. *The Early Middle Ages*. Austin, Texas: Steck-Vaughn Company, 1992.
Dambrosio, Monica, and Roberto Barbieri. *The Late Middle Ages*. Austin, Texas: Steck-Vaughn Company, 1992.
Hillyer, V. M., and E. G. Huey. *The Medieval World*. New York: Meredith Press, 1966.
Langley, Andrew. *Medieval Life*. New York: Alfred A. Knopf, 1996.
Macdonald, Fiona. *A Medieval Castle*. New York: Peter Bedrick Books, 1990.
Reid, Struan. *Castle*. New York: Barnes & Noble Books, 1996.

Books for Adults

Editors of Time-Life Books. *What Life Was Like in the Age of Chivalry: Medieval Europe A.D. 800–1500*. Alexandria, Virginia: Time Life, Inc., 1997.
Nicolle, David. *The Medieval World*. New York: Barnes & Noble Books, 1997.
Robards, Brooks. *The Medieval Knight*. New York: Barnes & Noble Books, 1997.

From *Everyday Life: The Middle Ages* © 2006 Good Year Books.